Afghanistan

Second edition

Chris Johnson

Oxfam

First published by Oxfam UK and Ireland in 1998
(0 85598 385 X)
Reprinted by Oxfam GB in 2002

Second edition published by Oxfam GB in 2004
(0 85598 503 8)

Available from:
Bournemouth English Book Centre, PO Box 1496, Parkstone,
Dorset, BH12 3YD, UK
tel: +44 (0)1202 712933; fax: +44 (0)1202 712930;
email: oxfam@bebc.co.uk

USA: Stylus Publishing LLC, PO Box 605, Herndon, VA
20172-0605, USA
tel: +1 (0)703 661 1581; fax: +1 (0)703 661 1547;
email: styluspub@aol.com

For details of local agents and representatives in other countries,
consult our website: http://www.oxfam.org.uk/publications
or contact Oxfam Publishing, 274 Banbury Road,
Oxford OX2 7DZ, UK
tel: +44 (0)1865 311 311; fax: +44 (0)1865 312 600;
email: publish@oxfam.org.uk

Our website contains a fully searchable database of all our titles,
and facilities for secure on-line ordering.

Oxfam GB is a registered charity, no. 202 918, and is a
member of Oxfam International.

© Oxfam GB 2004

ISBN 0 85598 503 8

A catalogue record for this publication is available from the
British Library.

Printed by
Information Press, Eynsham

Contents

Introduction

The terrorist attacks in New York and Washington on 11 September 2001 thrust Afghanistan back on to the world stage. For many years it had been all but forgotten by the international community: a problem that the world preferred not to have to think about. The Taliban regime's repressive policies on women's rights had caused ripples of discontent in the West, and their harbouring of the Saudi-born militant Osama bin Laden had hardened the attitudes of the USA and its allies, but it was only when the towers of the World Trade Center collapsed into dust that international attention really focused on Afghanistan.

It is all too easy for the West to think of Afghanistan in the simplistic terms promoted by the mass media: as a land of 'fundamentalist tribesmen', armed, bearded, and turbaned, brutalised by war, and pursuing ancient hatreds with all the destructiveness of modern weaponry. But such facile images cloud the truth. This is a complex land with a rich history, and those who prefer the kalashnikov to the pen and the plough are not the majority, despite the havoc that they cause. Perhaps Afghanistan's biggest misfortune is to have been entangled for so many years in other people's politics: as a buffer state between the imperial powers of Russia and Britain in the nineteenth century; as a battleground for the twentieth-century struggle between the Soviet Union and the USA, and as a focus for regional political rivalries; and finally in the continuing conflict between the USA and al-Qa'eda.

The major powers, therefore, bear a responsibility for what has happened in Afghanistan. When the Soviet Union fell apart and the Cold War came to an end, the USA transferred its attention to other regions; but the people of one of the poorest countries in the world continued to suffer, their society and economy torn apart by forces set in motion by superpower hostilities. The Taliban's initial appeal to many Afghans was rooted in ordinary people's despair over the prevailing anarchy in their country, and in their longing for the security that the Taliban appeared to promise. But the Taliban's harsh and narrow interpretation of Islam did not accord comfortably with Afghan traditions and, as they became more and more influenced by foreigners, they became increasingly disliked within their own country.

◀ *A family on the move in Panjao district, Bamiyan province, 2003. The war-weary people of Afghanistan still face an uncertain future.*

With the end of the Taliban regime in 2001 came a chance for peace in Afghanistan. But it is only a chance. The government of Hamid Karzai exists only because it is protected by American military might, and most Afghans believe that if US support were withdrawn, the country would slide back into open warfare. Even now, the government is beset by factional struggles, while the largest single group – the Pashtuns – continue to feel marginalised from the current political settlement. Meanwhile, in the south and east of Afghanistan, the anti-government alliance of the Taliban, al-Qa'eda, and the ex-*mujahedin* commander, Hekmatyar, is becoming increasingly well organised and has rendered large areas extremely dangerous for the operations of international relief and development organisations.

Whether Afghanistan can find its way forward from this precarious position to a peaceful future is not only an issue of great concern to its war-weary people, but one which will have a profound effect on regional stability, and ultimately on global security.

▶ *Carrying fuel in Dai Kundi district, Uruzgan province*

CHRIS JOHNSON/OXFAM GB

Afghanistan: ancient and modern

▲ *Timurid tilework, restored to its former splendour, decorates the Friday Mosque in Herat.*

CHRIS JOHNSON/OXFAM GB

The fabric of Afghan society

Outside the shops in downtown Herat, richly coloured fabrics blow in the wind, their metallic threads glistening in the late afternoon sun. Down the alleyway are glimpsed the minarets of the city's wonderful 'Masjid-i Jami', the Friday Mosque. Here, more than any other city in Afghanistan, can be seen something of the country's glorious past, and the richness of its peoples and cultures. Built by the Ghorids in the year 1200 on the site of a tenth-century mosque, redecorated in lavish tilework by the Timurids in the fifteenth century, restored again in the middle of the twentieth, the mosque is one of the few of Afghanistan's architectural treasures to survive recent conflicts. It is, however, far more than just a monument. Slip off your shoes, enter through an archway, and walk along a cool stone passage to emerge into the great courtyard, and you cannot fail to see that it is part of a living religion, a sacred and much-used space where children come to read their schoolbooks and adults come to pray, to give or receive alms, to talk, or just to be.

Sitting on a crossroads between south, west, and central Asia, Afghanistan has drawn its cultural heritage from all of these regions. Under Alexander the Great, the art of Greece was fused with local tradition. Kushan nomads from Central Asia brought Buddhism and left the richness of Gandhara art. Then came the great dynasties of Islam: the Ghaznavids, Ghorids, Timurids, Moghuls, and Safavids. They all left extraordinary treasures, part of Afghanistan's ancient cultural heritage, expressed in architecture, in the decorative work of tiles and mosaics, in exquisite miniature paintings and calligraphy, and through intricate design and rich colour in carpets, rugs, and embroidery.

Women as well as men contributed to these traditions – mostly in the domestic domain, although some women also found their place in public life. Queen Gawhar Shad, for example, ruled over the Timurid Empire for 50 years. By the time she was murdered in 1457, she was more than 80 years old. Under her patronage, arts and architecture flourished. She commissioned the Musalla Complex in Herat, one of the most imposing and elegant structures in the whole of South Asia, with mosaics of glazed tiles which were said to have 'a taste and excellence of craftsmanship never excelled'. Little remains: in 1885 the British, coming close to war with the Russians in a boundary dispute in western Afghanistan, ordered the destruction of most of its buildings.

Arts and crafts

Zinda Jan, in Herat province, is the centre of Afghanistan's age-old silk industry. A villager who works in his family's silk business describes some of the complexities of the craft. *'From the beginning of this village we made silk. Everyone who has mulberry trees does. It is a family business. I inherited the trade from my father and my grandfather. The women look after the silkworms, which grow for 17 days. Then the worms are put out into the sun to kill them, so we can use the cocoon. If they emerge from the cocoon, the thread is broken and it is no good.'*

▼ An Afghan carpet, woven according to a rediscovered traditional design by members of a UNESCO-supported project

CHRIS JOHNSON/OXFAM GB

Once the worms have served their purpose, the work passes over to the men, who put the cocoons into large vats, from where the thread is drawn off into skeins of coarse silk. It is then sold to the merchants of Herat, who finish it and weave it. Much of it is still made into carpets, or the traditional six-metre lengths of turban silk, but a local organisation has worked with producers to develop a range of beautiful modern scarves which are admired and sought after in London and New York.

Afghanistan is famous for its carpets, both knotted and woven. As with all its crafts, styles and patterns vary greatly from one part of the country to another. At one end of the industry are poor households which save up the wool from their few animals for three or four years until they have enough to make one *gelim* (woven rug). They will then keep it until they need money, when it will be sold: a shrewd strategy in a country where there are no banks in rural areas, and where until recently inflation would have rapidly reduced the value of any cash. At the other end of the spectrum is the well-organised industry that makes high-quality carpets for international

CHRIS JOHNSON/OXFAM GB

▲ *Women weaving a rug in Panjao district, Bamiyan province*

▼ *Haji Baz Gul, a famous musician, storyteller, and poet*

markets. Here too the weaving is often done as a household activity, but the wool will often be bought in, from as far away as Belgium and, more recently, New Zealand. Each type of carpet uses a particular type of wool. The dyes often come from Germany. Wool is often sent to Pakistan to be dyed and spun – even when it is local wool, which is then transported back to the original village or town for weaving. Most high-quality knotted carpets are not finished locally, but are 'cut' (the process of trimming the pile to a uniform height) elsewhere, often in Pakistan. In some areas it is often difficult to buy a carpet locally, because the whole production is geared to the export trade.

Poetry and song

Afghanistan's culture is expressed not only in its arts and crafts, but also in a strong oral tradition of poetry and song which existed before, and later alongside, the written word. It carried customs and taught values, and it spoke of love and longing.

It still lives on, although in recent years many writers were persecuted and even killed for their words, and poetry often became an expression of grief. Music also came under attack. But a people's culture cannot be banned all that easily: even when life seemed unbearably bleak, the spirit of resistance survived through the rich satirical humour of Afghan story-telling.

Islam

Culture is more than what a society makes: it is also a matter of how it lives. In Afghanistan, Islam is the common denominator in an otherwise very diverse society: the one component of identity that is shared by almost all Afghans, providing a common frame of reference for morality, rights, and obligations. Yet, like all religions, Islam has many variants, and its divisions have often increased tensions in society.

Like the other major monotheistic religions, Islam originated in the Middle East. Its key tenet is that '*There is no God but the One God, Allah, and Mohammed is his prophet.*' It follows in the tradition of Judaism and Christianity, with Mohammed revered as the last prophet. Islam consists of two major sects – Sunni and Shia – each of which is further sub-divided into various schools of belief. The split between the Sunni and Shia branches occurred in AD 658, in a dispute over the succession to the Caliph, or religious head. The Shia believe that he should be a descendant of the Prophet, while Sunnis believe that he should be chosen from the wider Muslim community. Over the centuries the Sunnis have tended to represent the establishment, while the Shia have been associated with more radical movements and a more liberal interpretation of the rights of women. It is usually Sunnis who have held state power in Islamic countries, although Iran is an exception. Most Muslims in Afghanistan belong to the Sunni tradition, but up to 20 per cent are Shi'ites.

▼ *The shrine of Hazrat Ali in Mazar-i Sharif, one of the holiest sites in Afghanistan*

CHRIS JOHNSON/OXFAM GB

▶ *Islam is an esssential element of daily life in Afghanistan, both in cities (opposite) and in rural areas, such as the village of Khamestana, with its own local shrine.*

All Afghan rulers have had, to some degree, to base their claim to legitimacy on Islam. Even those who initially tried to do otherwise later changed course. And because religious authority was both decentralised and very diverse, the state was always able to find scholars who were prepared to endorse its policies as being in accordance with Islam. At another level in people's consciousness, more deeply rooted and enduring, lies the popular notion of what an Islamic society should be, shaped by ethical and spiritual values that are passed down through generations in an oral tradition. The images and stories used to transmit this model can be readily mobilised for social action (as they were against the occupying Soviet forces during the 1980s), and they can co-exist with other myths and traditions, even older and more fundamental, rooted in tribal history and structure, which have proved far stronger and more enduring than modern concepts of nationalism.

Fundamental to Islam is the concept of a closely knit community, the 'community of believers', whose function is to enjoin good and forbid evil: a model which is held to be the ideal social organisation for humanity. Religious beliefs and customs permeate this society: social order is seen to be of divine origin, the ruler derives his authority from spiritual power, and political leadership is exercised according to religious law and tradition. Rulers are believed to rule with the sanction of Allah — a sanction which will be withdrawn if they violate Islam. The object of *jihad*, the 'holy war' against the infidel, is not to convert individuals to Islam, but rather to gain control over the affairs of societies in order to run them in accordance with Islamic principles.

In Afghanistan, religious authority has traditionally been based on three criteria: spiritual knowledge; sacred descent; and mystical association. The first of these is embodied in the scholars (*ulama*), trained at a *madrasa* (religious school) according to a set curriculum. They lead prayers and may themselves become judges or *madrasa* teachers. The second source of authority is found in its most prestigious form in the *sayyid*, descendants of the Prophet, serving as teachers, healers, and mediators. The third comes from the relationship between a spiritual guide or master and his pupils, institutionalised in the *sufi* brotherhoods. Prominent religious leaders often combine all three forms of authority. For many centuries, all learning and education took place within a religious framework, so every educated person was imbued with Islamic values, and all public appointments required religious education. Religious leaders, both Sunni and Shia, have extensive personal networks which link them to particular groups in Afghan society and extend into the wider Islamic world: students often attend centres of religious learning outside Afghanistan.

In the 1960s and 1970s, an Islamist movement emerged in opposition to the way in which the state conducted its affairs. Unlike the traditionalist religious parties, the Islamists saw the need for a broad revolutionary movement, leading to a transformation of Afghan society. The leaders of the Islamist resistance groups derived much of their influence from their legitimacy as champions of Islam, a legitimacy gained from their early involvement in the struggle against the Communist regime – and later lost as a result of their lawless behaviour. The Taliban in their turn claimed ultimate moral authority, yet many Afghans did not recognise the version of Islam that they proclaimed, and many felt great sadness for the way in which their harsh doctrines gave Islam a bad name.

Collective identities

Language, kinship, and common history also help to determine people's identity. What this means is different to different Afghans: urban or rural, north or south, male or female, young or old – all these aspects, and more, combine to determine each Afghan's sense of self. 'Ethnic groups' are essentially fluid social categories; their membership, distribution, and culture can (and do) change over time. While a quarter of a century of conflict has certainly sharpened ethnic divisions, the country's wars have never really been caused by ethnic hatred, and the ever-shifting political and military alliances easily cross ethnic boundaries. Even in rural areas, where a sense of group identity tends to be much stronger than in towns, ethnicity of itself was not a cause for strife, and conflict was equally likely to exist within a group as between groups. Nowadays, however, an increasing emphasis on ethnicity has dismayed many of the country's educated citizens, who still see themselves as 'Afghans', rather than as Pashtun, Tajik, or Hazara: they say that it is the politicians who have divided the people, in order to rule them.

▲ *Buzkashi: a traditional game, rather like polo. Played on horseback, it was probably brought to the area by Genghis Khan's Mongol warriors in the twelfth century*

Although there has never been a full census in Afghanistan, and all figures are much disputed, nevertheless most people agree that Pashtuns are the largest group, although not a majority. They can claim to be the founders of the Afghan kingdom and they were dominant since the formation of a Pashtun monarchy in the mid-eighteenth century until the time of the Rabbani–Massoud government of the early 1990s. From the mid-nineteenth century onwards, Pashtun dominance became extended and entrenched. Members of Pashtun tribes who had rebelled against the government and been defeated were forced to settle in the north of the country; while those who had aided the government in their struggle to subjugate the Hazaras were rewarded with grazing rights and trading opportunities in Hazarajat. Nation building therefore came to be seen as a process of 'Pashtunisation', with non-Pashtuns unable to compete on equal terms.

Pashtuns are divided into tribes and sub-tribes, each of which was traditionally isolated within its own boundaries. Their society is structured by the Pashtun code, *Pashtunwali*. Interference in each other's affairs has caused conflict between tribes throughout history, although interference by outsiders tends to create instant unity.

Tajiks are the next-largest group. Unlike the Pashtuns, they are not organised along tribal lines. Most Tajiks are Sunni Muslim and Persian-speaking, although the designation includes some sub-groups who are neither. They have tended to predominate in public services and government ministries, and they comprise the majority of the educated elite. As many Tajiks have considerable wealth, they have exerted significant political influence in the country's affairs.

The Hazaras live mainly in the central highlands, where they settled at least as far back as the thirteenth century. Their language, Hazaragi, is a Persian dialect, and most of them belong to the Shia branch of Islam. They have always lived on the edge of economic survival. From the 1880s onwards, the Hazaras suffered severe economic, political, and social repression.

Harsh living conditions – long winters, short agricultural seasons, poor roads – drove many to migrate to towns, especially Kabul, where they found employment as unskilled labourers and domestic workers.

The Uzbeks and Turkmen are the two largest Turkic groups in Afghanistan. Many were originally refugees from Soviet or Tsarist rule, and there are large populations in the central Asian republics. Many Uzbeks and Turkmen communities still live on the plains north of the Hindu Kush, where most of Afghanistan's arable land is found. They have tended to remain relatively independent of the central state. Other smaller groups include Nuristanis and Baluch.

In addition to these settled groups (some of whom travel with their flocks for part of the year), there are the *kuchis*, or nomads. The 1978 census put their number at half a million; but even before the recent drought which devastated their flocks, it was estimated that there were probably fewer than 100,000. *Kuchis* have diversified their livelihoods over the years, and while some remain dependent on their livestock, some of those with the largest herds are also powerful truckers, traders, and smugglers.

▼ *A billboard advertising 'Pine Lites' cigarettes, Kabul, 2003: multinational companies wasted no time in moving in after the fall of the Taliban.*

Social structures

In Afghanistan the social divide between town and village is still great. There are few cities, and until recently they exerted very little influence over social life in rural areas, although there are many economic links between them. However, since the fall of the Taliban in 2001, the cash generated by the opium trade, combined with a huge drop in the price of generators and satellite dishes, has brought foreign TV to many rural areas for the first time; the impact of this, along with the return of refugees from surrounding countries, is as yet unclear.

The basic unit of social organisation in rural areas is known as the *qawm*. The term is used to denote a variety of groups: various levels of tribal organisation; or people living in a specific area, such as a village or valley; or sometimes an occupational group. It is the village *qawm* which for most people defines their identity and allegiances. Rural Afghanistan consists of a patchwork of these, each representing a local landowning descent group. New *qawms* tend to form when an individual gains fame and importance, and he and his followers break away from their original social group and develop a separate identity.

Social organisation has become much less strong in the urban areas. In the 1980s the cities became bulwarks of the Communist regime, and the large civil service and a comprehensive system of state-provided rations inevitably changed the nature of social relationships. Later, food rations from international organisations filled much the same role. The lack of a sense of community is at its strongest in Kabul, where huge numbers of citizens have been displaced, both within the city and into the city from the rural areas, and people often no longer know their neighbours. In other cities there is a greater sense of community, though still far less evident than in most rural areas or small towns. Although the system of *wakils*, who are heads of *gozars* (sub-districts), in theory still exists, in practice these people's degree of popular legitimacy is limited.

Common ethnic identity does not necessarily result in political alliance. Relations are influenced by particular interests and concerns at a number of levels, and in consequence political alignments vary considerably between regions and over time. Disputes over land and other matters can easily lead to groups who share the same ethnic identity confronting each other as enemies, and where this happens they often enlist people belonging to other ethnic groups as their allies. Splits within *qawms* are common, especially because land is everywhere a scarce resource and thus readily becomes a source of conflict. The fluidity and complexity of social and political relations in Afghanistan have shaped the history of the country for centuries, and will continue to do so.

▼ *The sense of community is still strong in rural areas, as here among this group, gathered round the village well in Zinda Jan district, Herat province.*

CHRIS JOHNSON/OXFAM GB

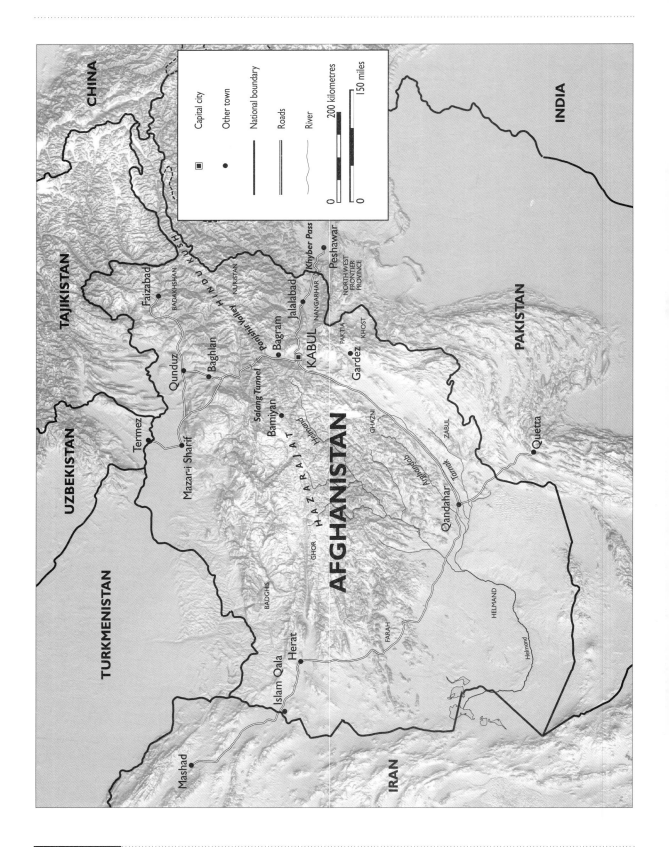

CHINA

INDIA

Capital city
Other town
National boundary
Roads
River

200 kilometres
150 miles

0
0

TAJIKISTAN

Faizabad

Peshawar

Khyber Pass

Jalalabad

NANGARHAR

NORTH-WEST
FRONTIER
PROVINCE

PAKISTAN

Baghlan

NURISTAN

Bagram

KABUL

PAKTIA

Qunduz

Salang Tunnel

Gardez

KHOST

Termez

Bamiyan

Helmand

GHAZNI

ZABUL

UZBEKISTAN

Mazar-i Sharif

HAZARAJAT

AFGHANISTAN

Arghandab

Tarnak

Quetta

GHOR

Qandahar

BADGHIS

HELMAND

Islam Qala

Herat

FARAH

Helmand

TURKMENISTAN

Mashad

IRAN

Imperial chess games

CHRIS JOHNSON/OXFAM GB

▲ *Carved 1700 years ago and destroyed by the Taliban in 2001, this 55-metre statue was a legacy of the Buddhist kingdom of Bamiyan.*

◄ *Map of Afghanistan, showing places featured in this book*

The area which is now Afghanistan has long been a borderland between empires, and for at least 2500 years its fortunes have often been determined by other people's battles. Parts of Afghanistan were included in the Persian empire of Darius the Great (522–486 BC) and the Hellenic empire of Alexander the Great (356–323 BC). After Alexander's empire broke up, the area became a patchwork of Greek dynasties and city-states; many present-day towns are built on Greek foundations. In the late first to mid-fifth centuries AD, a Buddhist civilisation flourished, centred at Gandhara; Buddhist kings reigned in Bamiyan until the end of the tenth century. Islam arrived with the first Arab (Muslim) raid on Qandahar in 699–700 and spread thereafter, being consolidated in the Ghaznavid period (977–1186), when the Turks began to gain power in Iran, Afghanistan, and India. The famous Silk Route between China and Europe passed through the area. The land was conquered by Genghis Khan in the thirteenth century, and was subsequently fought over by the empires of India and Persia. When in the eighteenth century the power of these countries waned, a group of Pashtun tribes under Durrani founded their own empire; like other tribal empires, it proved unstable.

Of Britain, Russia, and the consolidation of a state ...

During the nineteenth century the British, mistrusting Russian intentions in the region, tried to bring Afghanistan under direct rule. The first Anglo-Afghan war (1839–1842) ended in disastrous defeat for Britain. The second (1878–1880) left Afghanistan maintaining its internal sovereignty, but ceding control of its external affairs to Britain. The British then sought to keep the Russians at bay and to create a stable north-west frontier for their Indian empire, by providing modern weapons and an annual subsidy to Afghanistan's rulers. The resources were used by the Pashtun rulers to establish state control and manipulate social divisions in order to weaken resistance to their regime. It was the beginning of a system which in its essentials was to last until the end of the Najibullah regime in 1992 and the consequent disintegration of the Afghan state.

The person most responsible for turning Afghanistan from a tribal confederacy into a centralised state was Abdul Rahman Khan (1881–1901). British cash enabled him to create a well-equipped army, which he used ruthlessly to crush internal dissent and consolidate the state. However, the tribal areas retained a measure of independence and were never brought totally under central control. Moreover, attempts to build a modern state did not extend to the creation of a national market or links to world markets, partly because of a fear that such developments would open up Afghanistan to outside interference, with subsequent loss of independence. The country therefore remained economically isolated.

▼ Afghanistan was isolated from the rest of the world for centuries by its remote, rugged terrain and by the policies of successive rulers.

CHRIS JOHNSON/OXFAM GB

Abdul Rahman Khan died in 1901 and was replaced by his son Habibullah, in a peaceful succession that was without precedent in the history of Afghanistan. Habibullah continued to pursue many of the policies of his father, but with the important difference that he introduced a modern style of education, thus enabling a class of intellectuals to develop, separate from the clergy.

In the wake of the First World War, pressure mounted within Afghanistan for independence from the British, and Habibullah's continuing co-operation with them resulted in his assassination in 1919. After a short power struggle, his son, Amanullah, seized the throne and declared independence. This was immediately recognised by Russia; after a brief war, the British conceded defeat. Amanullah tried hard to transform

▲ *Kabul, December 2001:
the building in the background
is the Royal Palace, a relic of
the former splendour of the
war-devastated city.*

Afghanistan into a modern nation state, reversing previous isolationist economic policies and opening up the country to trade. He undertook land reform, regularised taxes, improved roads, extended education, and, in 1921, gave the country its first constitution. But his attempts to shift power away from village elders and the religious establishment led to revolts which toppled him in 1928.

The first of the revolts to reach Kabul was led by Bacha-yi-Saqao ('Son of the Water Carrier'), a Tajik bandit from the north. However, after a reign of less than a year he was deposed by Nadir Khan, eldest of the Pashtun Musahiban brothers. Thus began a dynasty which lasted until 1978. Nadir Shah (*shah* means 'king') shared to some extent the ideal of modernising Afghanistan, but tribal society was still strong, and the state was weak. Instead he compromised, using external funds to build a modern state sector in Kabul which excluded the rural power holders but left them with a large measure of local autonomy. Assassinated in 1933, he was succeeded by his 19-year-old son, Mohammed Zahir. For the first twenty years, Zahir Shah's reign was controlled by his two uncles, as successive prime ministers. The first ruled autocratically; the second ushered in what became known as the 'Liberal Parliament', which sat from 1949 until 1952, when Zahir Shah's cousin, Daoud, seized control as Prime Minister. In 1963, Zahir Shah asserted his own authority and tried to develop a constitutional monarchy under what became known as the New Democracy.

Under both the Liberal Parliament of 1949–1952 and New Democracy of 1964–1973, intellectuals enjoyed considerable freedom; at other times they suffered imprisonment and exile. They were never able to exert much influence on the state. Zahir Shah's decision in 1963 to introduce a more representative form of government was a recognition that the state needed legitimacy among both the intellectuals and the traditional power structures; and the new constitution, introduced in 1964, provided for elected upper and lower houses of a consultative parliament. (The boundaries of the districts were set in order to ensure Pashtun dominance.) But the legislation permitting the existence of political parties was never actually signed, and the king retained control over the government, which was neither selected from, nor responsible to, parliament. Parliament was seen not as an institution for nation-wide democracy, but as a means of gaining legitimacy and support in the countryside.

Many university graduates found jobs in the army or state bureaucracy, rendering the state more independent of tribal power structures. Nevertheless, the strategy of Afghanistan's rulers was still to fragment tribal power and manoeuvre round it, rather than confront it. At village level, people continued to rely on local power networks, and the state had little authority.

In 1973 the former Prime Minister Daoud staged a coup, proclaiming Afghanistan a republic and himself as its President. The coup signalled a change in the struggle for power, for Daoud seized control not as head of a tribal army but as leader of a group of Soviet-trained military officers. During his brief rule, the country benefited from increased revenues from natural gas and from higher remittances sent back by Afghans working in the Gulf states. It also began to receive aid from Iran, as Daoud sought to increase Afghanistan's independence by playing off donors against each other. Supported by external funding, Daoud's government had little incentive to make itself accountable to the people.

Time for change

Several parallel developments were now beginning to erode the foundations of the old order. Kabul was full of students experiencing for the first time the dislocation between their rural, traditional backgrounds and life in a big city. Kabul University became a hot-bed of ideas — both Communist and Islamic — as men and women from all over the country mixed together (the university became co-educational in 1960) and encountered foreign teachers. It was the students from those days who were to provide the leadership in the war to come. Agricultural modernisation, combined with the oil boom of the early 1970s, encouraged the migration of labour on a scale which altered patterns of social control and exposed many less educated people to new ideas.

The Sawr Revolution, 1978

The time for change had come. The principal Communist organisation in Afghanistan, the People's Democratic Party of Afghanistan (PDPA), which by now had effectively penetrated the military, began planning a coup.

It succeeded in overthrowing Daoud in the Sawr Revolution of 27 April 1978. The PDPA had been founded in 1965, split into two factions (PDPA-Khalq and PDPA-Parcham) in 1967, and reunited again in 1977. Shortly after it took power, conflict again broke out within the party, and all the Parcham leaders were expelled. PDPA-Khalq, a small group of intellectuals with little popular support and no means of relating to the rural community, pushed forward its ideas by decree and force. Its attack on Islam and its ties to the USSR further undermined its legitimacy.

Between 1978 and 1979, the regime's programme of radical reforms provoked local rebellions, and at the same time a whole series of army insurrections took place. Although these were suppressed, each brought a defection of troops to join the escaped leaders of the revolts. Afghanistan was of too much strategic importance to be left alone. In the months following the Sawr Revolution, the USSR, reluctant to see the disintegration of a Communist regime on its doorstep, increased aid to the Afghan government. A friendship treaty signed by the Taraki government and the USSR in 1978 prompted the USA and other Western states to begin actively supporting the various resistance groups that eventually coalesced into 'the *mujahedin*'. When the Taraki government fell, the subsequent Karmal regime refused to moderate its policies or to seek coalition partners. This alienated its Soviet backers, and, alarmed by the growing disorder and fearful of US attempts to regain in Afghanistan the influence that it had lost in Iran, Soviet President Brezhnev sent troops south across the border in December 1979.

▶ *A Russian gun emplacement overlooking the outskirts of Kabul*

JENNY MATTHEWS/OXFAM GB

The Soviet occupation, 1979–1989

Believing that if its policies were modified, people would accept the Communist regime, the Soviets had initially planned to withdraw from Afghanistan after six months. Babrak Karmal, leader of the Parcham faction, was brought back to lead the government, and the most unpopular policies were changed. Prisoners were released, and an amnesty for refugees was announced; literacy classes were segregated by sex and made strictly voluntary for women; and the regime declared its allegiance to Islam. The strategy failed: the presence of foreign troops on Afghan soil caused localised resistance to evolve into nation-wide uprising. Starting with a mutiny in the Herat garrison, revolt quickly spread.

Before the Soviet invasion, the resistance to the Communist government had been spontaneous and under local leadership. Political parties were rarely involved, and external aid was minimal, although Pakistan supplied some small weapons. Villagers had little sense of nationhood and interpreted the call to *jihad* — the defence of Islam and the liberation of the land — in local terms. At this stage the 'armed forces' consisted in effect of the entire population under arms, and fighting was often interrupted for economic activities, such as planting and harvesting. The needs of the *mujahedin* ('fighters in a holy war') in these early years were largely supplied by Islamic taxes and other sources of local income, and a resistance unit consisted simply of a commander and his men.

▼ *A mujahedin commander beside an abandoned Russian tank, 1996*

JENNY MATTHEWS/OXFAM GB

After the Soviet invasion the resistance movement began to change. In Peshawar, the seven exiled Sunni parties gained recognition from Pakistan (which controlled the increasing flows of aid from the USA, Saudi Arabia, and China), and tens of thousands of fighters received military training. Pakistan, not wishing to see a united Afghan resistance movement on its soil which might threaten its own control over Afghan refugees and the conduct of the war, pursued a policy which encouraged dissension among the Peshawar-based parties. As foreign funding and opium money enabled resistance units to grow more autonomous, so various forms of radical fundamentalism flourished.

Increased military pressure forced local leaders in Afghanistan to turn to exiled parties for arms; weapons were in short supply, although volunteers were plentiful. As aid increased, the *mujahedin* became less dependent on the local population and took to living in military camps, rather than their homes. The Soviet forces destroyed agriculture and livestock, to make it harder for people to supply the *mujahedin*. The war changed social structures, as the traditional landed elite gave place to new power-holders: the commanders.

The Soviet army and air-force relied on the force of arms to suppress rural insurgency; their indiscriminate bombing of villages killed nearly one million people, while KhAD, the KGB-organised secret police, imposed terror on urban areas. The numbers of Soviet troops quickly grew to exceed 100,000, far outnumbering the army of Afghanistan, which was reduced in numbers by desertions. Yet a military stalemate developed, with the government controlling Kabul and other major towns, and the resistance operating freely in most of the countryside.

Until the mid-1980s the Soviets virtually controlled the Afghan state structure; all major offices were staffed with Soviet advisers; in economic terms, government-controlled Afghanistan became a Soviet republic. The USSR paid the government's deficits and gave financial and technical assistance for state investment. Afghanistan's natural-gas supplies, developed with Soviet money and expertise, were sold directly to the USSR. Taxes became impossible to collect in the countryside, which forced the regime into further reliance on the Soviets. Because the war had created shortages of food and fuel in Kabul, for many years the Soviets provided 100,000 tons of wheat annually as a gift, and the same amount again in exchange for goods. The occupation was costing the Soviets about $5 billion a year, but they never committed the troops necessary to gain a decisive military victory over the *mujahedin*. The Americans, meanwhile, determined to make Afghanistan the USSR's Vietnam, poured in weapons to arm the opposition.

Soviet withdrawal

By the time that Mikhail Gorbachev became Soviet President in March 1985, it had become clear that propping up the PDPA government in Afghanistan was a long-term and costly endeavour. Gorbachev gave the Afghan leadership and his own military one year to make decisive progress. When they failed, he changed course.

Considering this ultimatum to the military, it was perhaps not surprising that the final year was the bloodiest of the war. However, it brought no success for the Soviets; weakened by diminishing resources at home and increasing resistance in Afghanistan, Gorbachev and the Soviet leadership opted for compromise and withdrawal. In November 1986, they decided to withdraw the troops by the end of 1988. Meanwhile they would work to establish a friendly, neutral government in Afghanistan. The USA, refusing to believe that Gorbachev was serious in his intentions to withdraw, continued to equip the opposition forces.

As part of the attempt to create a more acceptable government, Karmal was exiled in November 1987, and Najibullah, head of KhAD, the Afghan Intelligence Service, took over as President. Under pressure from the Soviets to promote reconciliation, he spent the next four years presiding over the reversal of virtually every aspect of the state's previous policies. Amendments to the constitution provided for devolution of some control to local power structures — in effect, recognising the power held by resistance commanders — and the government tried to set up commissions of national reconciliation at the local level. These commissions had the right to appoint democratic structures of local government, the first time such a thing had happened in Afghanistan; but, as nomination to a commission often resulted in execution by the resistance, little significant progress was made.

All of Gorbachev's attempts to organise negotiations on the transfer of power failed. With no solution in sight, the Soviets agreed to withdraw their troops under the Geneva Accords, signed on 14 April 1988. Withdrawal began in the next month and was completed in February the following year.

▼ Between 1986 and 1990, weapons worth $5 billion were supplied to the mujahedin.

SEAN SUTTON/OXFAM GB

International involvement in Afghanistan

Even before the Soviet invasion, international aid had distorted the political and economic development of Afghanistan. From 1956 to 1973, foreign grants and loans accounted for 80 per cent of the country's investment and development expenditure. This relieved the government of the need to build up a domestic taxation base and so reduced the need to establish governmental structures to control the country. The members of the political elite neither organised the people nor represented their interests: far from attempting to govern effectively, they simply acted as one link in a chain of patronage. The Afghan people related to their government by using kinship connections to obtain favours and privileges.

From 1958 to 1964 more than half the aid was spent on improving transport facilities, mainly by the construction of all-weather roads and airports — an infrastructure which, ironically, made the Soviet invasion of 1979 possible. It also encouraged labour migration, both within Afghanistan and externally to oil-rich Iran, bringing about social change which later had political repercussions. Towards the end of the 1960s, agriculture came to dominate spending, with wheat production subsidised by investment in large (and often wasteful) irrigation projects. The most pernicious effect of aid, however, was to provide cash and weapons for a modern army and police force, with which the government – in the absence of other means – controlled the people.

During the Cold War, the strategic significance of Afghanistan meant that both the USSR and the USA poured aid into the country. Between 1955 and 1978, the USSR gave $2.52 billion, and the USA gave $533 million. By the late 1980s, aid from the USA and Saudi Arabia combined reached about $1bn per year. The UK, China, Pakistan, and others also contributed. In addition, between 1986 and 1990 weapons worth about $5bn were sent to the *mujahedin*, especially, from September 1986, shoulder-held Stinger anti-aircraft missiles to counteract Soviet HIND helicopter gunships. Conversely, weapons worth $5.7m were supplied to the Kabul regime. Afghanistan was now importing weapons on the same scale as Saudi Arabia. By 1992 the country was estimated to have more weapons in private ownership than India and Pakistan combined.

There was little co-ordination between the various external funders. Military aid to the *mujahedin* tended to be given according to the degree of damage inflicted on the Soviets – a fact which encouraged extremist groups. Because funders favoured the parties in exile, internal groups were forced into alliances with them in order to obtain arms. The consequences for a peaceful political solution to Afghanistan's problems were ignored. Humanitarian assistance, meanwhile, was closely tied to Western efforts to bring about Soviet withdrawal and the collapse of the Communist regime. Aid was used to provide services and support the livelihoods of groups living in *mujahedin* areas. In the period 1986–1990, for example, USAID spent $150m on health care, agriculture, and education. Much of the assistance was channelled through non-government organisations (NGOs), whose operations reinforced the fragmentation of Afghanistan, as a policy of delivering aid directly to rural areas via commanders built up local power bases.

The struggle for power continues

When Soviet troops finally withdrew in 1989, the USA believed that the Afghan government would quickly fall. It was not to be. Najibullah could play the nationalist card (in contrast to the resistance forces, which were backed by Pakistan and Saudi Arabia), while using Soviet aid to play off his antagonists, one against the other. In this way he survived for a further three years, but despite the fact that the government began to offer autonomy, political recognition, and Soviet-supplied goods to those commanders who would abandon their opposition, state control over rural areas was minimal. Too weak to create an effective military force, the government relied on local militias to keep communications open between the cities. Its liberalisation measures failed to halt the economic decline. The aid that Najibullah received did not compensate for the withdrawal of troops. He needed more money, which was printed for him in Russia; the result was hyper-inflation.

Once the Soviet forces had left, the *mujahedin* were able to capture large parts of Afghanistan; but the fragmented nature of the resistance, with shifting loyalties and rivalries, meant that they were unable to turn these local victories into a national one. The one unifying factor, *jihad*, had disappeared along with the Soviet troops, and little was left but a raw struggle for power. Iran, increasingly concerned about Pakistan's dominance in Afghanistan, put pressure on the Shias to form a single party, Hizb-i-Wahdat, to which it channelled all its aid. The Sunni parties continued to be bitterly divided. As the Soviet threat waned, so too did American interest. There was no real commitment to finding a long-term political solution.

▼ *In 1994, there were some 700 tanks in Kabul, and they were almost as common as cars on the city's streets*

SEAN SUTTON/OXFAM GB

SEAN SUTTON/OXFAM GB

▲ Mujahedin *loyal to Rabbani watch from their vantage point in the ruins of Darulaman Palace, on the outskirts of Kabul, 1994.*

Throughout the summer of 1991 the UN attempted to mediate, but it proved impossible to get all parties even to meet together, let alone agree to anything. In March 1992, Najibullah announced that he would leave office as soon as a transitional authority was formed. The resulting power vacuum increased the conflict. Afghanistan was breaking apart. As Soviet aid dwindled, the northern militias under the command of General Dostum deserted the government and joined forces with the northern *mujahedin*. Fearing that the state would disintegrate totally, the UN put pressure on the various parties to reach a settlement. Najibullah prepared to depart on a UN plane, which would also fly the members of an interim government into Kabul from Peshawar. However, he was stopped at a checkpoint on the way to the airport and fled to the UN compound, where he was given refuge.

With the leaders in Peshawar still divided, the forces of Dostum and Ahmad Shah Massoud entered Kabul in order to prevent a takeover of the city by the Hizb-i Islami leader Gulbuddin Hekmatyar and his allies. As the rival forces battled for the city, party leaders, excluding Hekmatyar, signed the Peshawar Accords. An interim government took office, but the Accords were never fully implemented and they brought no peace. The government had little power and virtually no money. Customs posts, the major sources of income, remained in the hands of regional commanders. Four main groups (the forces of Dostum, Rabbani/Massoud, Hekmatyar, and Mazari of Hizb-i Wahdat), each with their own foreign backers, fought for control of Kabul.

► July 1994: a scene of devastation in Kabul, where an estimated 20,000 people died during the struggle for power among the mujahedin.

SEAN SUTTON/OXFAM GB

▼ Just one of the countless casualties of the civil war. Tariq picked up something that looked like a pen, but it was a mine and it exploded. He was wounded in the abdomen, and his right hand had to be amputated.

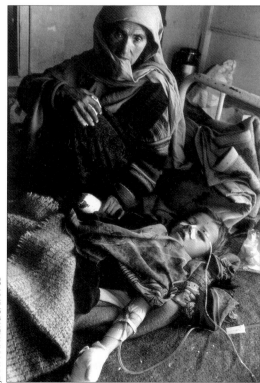

JENNY MATTHEWS/OXFAM GB

Fighting intensified throughout the summer of 1992. As Hekmatyar's rockets slammed into the city, and Iranian-backed Shia fought against the forces of Sayyaf and other Arab-backed Sunnis, waves of refugees left for Jalalabad and Pakistan. In August, the UN reported that more than 1800 civilians had been killed, food was becoming scarce, and some 500,000 people were fleeing the city. By the end of 1992, Kabul was devastated; the casualty total had risen to 5000 dead and about one million displaced, either within Afghanistan or as refugees in Pakistan.

New international diplomatic efforts resulted in the Islamabad Accords of March 1993, an agreement which declared sworn enemies Rabbani and Hekmatyar as President and Prime Minister respectively. It did nothing to resolve the problems. In January 1994 a new offensive destroyed further areas of Kabul, and more refugees fled from the city. By the end of that year, conservative estimates, based on the numbers of casualties arriving at Kabul hospitals, suggested that more than 20,000 people had died since Najibullah stepped down from power.

By this time most Afghans were desperate for peace. When, in 1994, the members of a UN mission travelled around the country, thousands turned out to meet them and to demand that the UN (which had by this time virtually dropped Afghanistan from its political agenda) should make renewed efforts to negotiate a peace settlement. The leaders of the warring factions refused even to meet with each other.

Enter the Taliban

At this point a new force entered the arena. The Taliban first made international news in November 1994, when they freed a Pakistani convoy which had been ambushed by local militia. They marched on Qandahar, where they met with little resistance, and took control of the city. Qandahar had previously been divided up among several commanders, and residents had suffered greatly at the hands of the militia. The Taliban imposed order, collected weapons, tore down the checkpoints set up to extort money, and refused to take bribes.

Well armed, and with public opinion on their side, the Taliban advanced throughout Afghanistan. Initially they encountered little opposition: the *mujahedin* either fled or joined them. Much of their support was born of disillusionment and despair: initially, many Afghans simply handed over their arms to what seemed an invincible force bent on a righteous cause. In September 1995 the Taliban captured the strategic city of Herat, and the following year Kabul. Ex-President Najibullah was taken from the UN compound, executed, and strung up for all to see.

From Kabul the Taliban advanced northwards. In May 1997 they attacked the northern capital of Mazar-i-Sharif, which they finally took in August 1998. In the course of the conflict, civilians and captured soldiers were massacred by both sides. The Taliban then moved on to take Bamiyan and Hazarajat, without much resistance. Further fighting took place in 1999, particularly in the Shamali Plain to the north of Kabul, in Dar-e Suf (a Hizb-i Wahdat enclave in the mountains between central Hazarajat and Mazar), and in Kwaja Ghar in the north-east.

Differing values

The name 'Taliban' means 'religious students', and the original members were traditional Islamic scholars from the southern Pashtun tribes, and students (both Afghan refugees and Pakistanis) studying in the Sunni *madrasas* of Pakistan. Their leader, Mohammed Omar, is a *mullah* (religious leader) from Qandahar and a former *mujahid*.

The values of the core of the Taliban movement were often said to be those of a Pashtun village, but this was a misrepresentation of rural Pashtun tradition. Rather, what was seen in the Taliban were village values as they were assumed to be by students who had been brought up in the isolation of a *madrasa* and had never really known village life. Their version of Islam was strict and dogmatic, and many Afghans did not recognise it as the religion that they loved. During their rule, a series of edicts was issued in an attempt to control all aspects of people's lives. They banned women from working outside the home (except in health care and a limited number of humanitarian projects), closed girls' schools, and insisted that men should grow full beards and pray five times a day. Television and the public playing of music were banned, and military checkpoints were adorned with yards of tape pulled from offending cassettes. However, implementation of their rules was far from universal. They were much stricter in the cities; in many

rural areas life went on much as it always had. Even in the cities, a number of prohibitions, such as the infamous one against flying kites, were issued and then quietly forgotten.

Reactions to Taliban rule were initially mixed. On the one hand, after 18 years of armed conflict, there was such a desperate longing for stability and peace that for some people almost any price was worth paying for some basic security. On the other hand, many people found their oppressive policies abhorrent. It was the educated city-dwellers, and particularly women, who were worst affected. In the Pashtun provinces of the east and south, the Taliban were on the whole welcomed, because once again it was possible to travel the roads safely, without the fear of encountering men with guns, and the Taliban made little difference to people's way of life, since much the same code was already in place. Even in rural Hazarajat, where people feared that they would be persecuted for their faith (Hazaras being followers of the Shi'ite rather than Sunni branch of Islam), little changed beyond the few areas where isolated fighting continued. Women who had never traditionally worn the *burqa* still did not wear it, people followed their religion in their own way, and communities and development agencies generally found it possible to negotiate the continuation of programmes with women.

JENNY MATTHEWS/OXFAM GB

JENNY MATTHEWS/OXFAM GB

SEAN SUTTON/OXFAM GB

As the Taliban expanded their control of Afghanistan and became the dominant force, with weapons and cash to distribute, their membership became more diverse. Pashtun youths from tribal areas, many of whom had no religious training, saw the movement as a means of re-asserting Pashtun power after the demise of the former Tajik-led government; and other groups simply joined the winning side. Then, as the Taliban began to find it difficult to make further military progress, there were increasing numbers of alliances of convenience and a greater reliance on foreign fighters. Both these factors tarnished the Taliban's image of purity. Even in many parts of the south and east, where once they had had support, people turned against them, motivated by resentment of military conscription and the Taliban's disregard for traditional authority, and also by anger at the increasing presence of foreign supporters of the regime, mostly from Pakistan but also in significant numbers from Chechnya and Uzbekistan. Some of the worst abuses of the war were committed by foreigners fighting alongside the Taliban, and these, together with increasing evidence of corruption, left many people to conclude that they were no better than those who had gone before them.

International intervention continues

The pattern of international interference in the affairs of Afghanistan continued in the Taliban years. Pakistan was widely reported to have provided funding, training, and diplomatic support, recruited fighters, given military advice, and provided shipments of fuel and ammunition. Between 1994 and 1999, an estimated 100,000 Pakistanis had trained and fought in Afghanistan, and as many as 30 trucks a day were said to have crossed the border, carrying artillery shells, tank rounds, and rocket-propelled grenades. Few seemed to grasp how dangerous this support would turn out to be for Pakistan itself, and the extent to which it would fuel Islamic militancy within its own borders.

◄ above: *A street in Kabul, viewed through the small meshed window of a burqa, the all-enveloping costume that women in most areas of Afghanistan were compelled to wear in public under Taliban rule.*

below: *Many women still do not feel safe to appear in public without the* burqa.

In the mid-1990s, Saudi Arabia too provided funds, goods, and diplomatic support. Official support eventually ceased, but private money from Saudi and other Gulf states continued to flow to the Taliban. The USA initially appeared to welcome the Taliban. Shortly after they took Kabul, Assistant Secretary of State, Robin Raphel, urged the world not to isolate them, saying: 'The Taliban control more than two thirds of the country, they are Afghan, they are indigenous, they have demonstrated staying-power.' Twice in 1997 Taliban representatives met with State Department officials in Washington. Behind this early policy position lay concerns about instability in Afghanistan, a wish to extend oil and gas pipelines across Afghanistan to the Black Sea, and a desire to reduce the influence of Iran and Russia in the region.

The Taliban were also to receive increasing support from Osama bin Laden. Born in 1957 in Saudi Arabia, the son of a Yemeni building contractor who had made a fortune in Saudi, Osama studied in Jedda. After the Soviet invasion, he made his way to Afghanistan to support the struggle of the *mujahedin*. He financed the recruitment, transport, and training of the Arab volunteers who flocked to fight in the *jihad*, and had close ties with both Hekmatyar and Sayyaf. Shortly after the withdrawal of Soviet troops, bin Laden left Afghanistan and returned to Saudi Arabia. He formed al-Qa'eda in 1985, with the aims of returning Muslim states to true Islamic governance, and of using violent means to remove foreign troops, and particularly US troops, from the holy places of Mecca and Medina in Saudi Arabia. The name *al-Qa'eda* means 'the base'. The organisation has a loose, cell-like structure and operates across a range of countries. As part of its global struggle it has supported several national radical Islamist movements, including the Taliban, which it came increasingly to influence. Deprived of Saudi citizenship in 1994, bin Laden settled in Sudan, where he remained until 1996, when he returned to Afghanistan.

Meanwhile, Iran, India, Russia, and the central Asian republics all gave support to the anti-Taliban forces. Their motives varied. India's support was prompted by its long-running struggle with Pakistan; for Iran, what mattered was the Sunni/Shia split within Islam and its desire to limit Saudi Arabia's influence in the Muslim world; for Russia and the central Asian republics, it was fear of the destabilising effect of the Taliban's presence near their borders, their interests in the oil and gas industry, and, in Russia's case, a desire to maintain something of its influence in this part of the world. Whatever the reason, sufficient money and arms poured in to Afghanistan to ensure that no one group could end the war by military means.

End game

By 2000 the Taliban controlled 90 per cent of Afghanistan, but they were still unrecognised by all but Saudi Arabia, Pakistan, and the United Arab Emirates; and to their chagrin, Rabbani still held Afghanistan's seat at the United Nations. Their harbouring of Osama bin Laden, whom the USA believed responsible for the bombing of its embassies in Nairobi and Dar-es-Salaam in 1998, along with an increasingly vociferous campaign mounted by prominent American feminists, had earned them the disapproval of the superpower, which was instrumental in bringing in two rounds of UN sanctions, the first at the end of 1999 and the second, and tougher, at the beginning of 2001. The USA had three demands: the end of support for terrorists; improvement in women's rights; and an end to the growing of opium poppy. The Taliban had always accused the West of double standards over women's rights, asking why there had been no condemnation of rapes and killings committed by the *mujahedin*; but it was the issue of opium that finally confirmed their conviction that the West was immutably opposed to them.

In February 2000, the Taliban had issued a ban on the growing of opium poppy, and the following year experts, including UN and US officials, agreed that the poppy had indeed been comprehensively eradicated from all the Taliban-controlled territory. (It was still being cultivated on a large scale in the province of Badakhshan, controlled by the Northern Alliance, a grouping of Afghan forces opposed to the Taliban.) The international community, however, failed to respond to Taliban requests for support with crop-substitution programmes, arguing that the ban was merely a ploy to reduce supplies and keep prices high.

Relations with the West continued to worsen, reaching a new low in February 2001 with the destruction of the famous Bamiyan Buddhas. The statues, standing 38 metres and 55 metres high respectively, dated from the third or very early fourth century AD and were carved into two niches in a mountain. Although they were much damaged by fighting, having been used as a military base by successive groups, they were still extraordinary monuments (see the picture on page 13). Only three months earlier, the Taliban had proclaimed that as part of Afghanistan's heritage they should be preserved; their subsequent savage destruction was seen by many as a measure of the deterioration in the relationship between the Taliban and the West: an act of iconoclasm which seemed to tell the world that the radical leadership in Afghanistan cared nothing for external opinion.

One more crucial event was to occur before September 11th 2001. On 9th September, some Arab journalists carrying Belgian passports arrived in the Panjshir Valley to conduct an interview with Ahmad Shah Massoud, the leader of the Northern Alliance. A bomb hidden in the cameraman's equipment exploded, killing Massoud. Suspicion immediately fell on Osama bin Laden.

▶ From warlord to national hero: the face of Massoud by the roadside on the edge of the Shamali Plain, north of Kabul

The impact of September 11th

When the hijacked planes struck the Pentagon and the World Trade Center on September 11th 2001, it was inevitable that Osama bin Laden would be held responsible, and equally certain that this would mean retaliation against the Taliban for giving him sanctuary. On 7th October, the USA launched 'Operation Enduring Freedom'. Determined not to be trapped in a long-running war in Afghanistan, it used massive air-power, operating in alliances with Northern Alliance forces, which were to do most of the fighting on the ground, with the support of Coalition Special Forces.

On 13th November the Taliban deserted Kabul, and the Northern Alliance walked into the city unopposed. The Taliban stronghold of Qandahar finally fell on 9th December. On 16th December, US Secretary of State Colin Powell announced: '*We've destroyed al-Qa'eda in Afghanistan, and we have ended the role of Afghanistan as a haven for terrorist activity*'. His words were to prove premature. For, while the al-Qa'eda leaders had certainly fled, probably into neighbouring Pakistan, the organisation's cell-based structure makes it remarkably difficult to destroy, and the long, undefended Afghan border is easy to infiltrate. It has become clear that the Taliban have been

▼ *A stone cairn in Baluchistan marks the official border between Pakistan and Afghanistan.*

ANNIE BUNGEROTH/OXFAM GB

able to regroup, in alliance with Gulbuddin Hekmatyar, the leader of Hizb-i Islami, and with the support of al-Qa'eda. They have been responsible for an increasing number of attacks on international forces and on aid-agency personnel.

By the time the Bonn Agreement was signed at the Inter-Afghan Conference in December 2001, some 12,000 bombs had been dropped on Afghanistan, including cluster bombs, each capable of scattering 200 bomblets over a wide area; these lie unexploded on or in the ground until disturbed. They are a significant hazard for civilians long after a war is over. Even worse was the fact that the cluster bombs were dropped in the areas where the US forces dropped food parcels, and both types of object were yellow. Due to the use of bomblets, the landmine-awareness programme had to be redesigned to include cluster bombs.

Afghans themselves had mixed feelings about the military campaign of the US-led Coalition. Most were delighted at the prospect of getting rid of the Taliban and believed that the superiority of US air-power would make the war quick and relatively painless. On the other hand, they were deeply concerned that the Afghan opposition forces with whom the USA had allied itself were the same people who were guilty of rape, murder, and extortion and whose rocket attacks had virtually destroyed Kabul in the mid-1990s.

The Bonn Agreement and the political process

At the end of November 2001, key representatives of the various Afghan interest groups met in Petersburg, near Bonn, along with senior diplomats from the United Nations. On 5th December they finally signed the 'Agreement on provisional arrangements in Afghanistan pending the re-establishment of permanent government institutions', more commonly known as 'The Bonn Agreement'. This provided for the setting up of an Afghanistan Interim Authority (AIA), to be followed within six months by the convening of an emergency *loya jirga* (grand assembly) to decide upon an Afghanistan Transitional Authority (ATA), including a broad-based transitional administration. A constitutional *loya jirga* was then to be held within 18 months of the establishment of the ATA, in order to adopt a new constitution. Finally, elections were due to be held no later than mid-2004. In support of the transition, a number of commissions were to be established: a Judicial Commission, a Constitutional Commission, a Civil Service Commission, and a Human Rights Commission. The formation of a multinational International Security Assistance Force (ISAF) was agreed, 'to assist in the maintenance of security for Kabul and its surrounding areas'.

Though often described as a peace agreement, the Bonn Agreement was in reality a deal brokered between victorious factions in the wake of a war won largely by an external power. The rivalries of the various groups making up the Northern Alliance remained unresolved, and the Shura-yi Nazar faction which walked into Kabul after Coalition forces had bombed the Taliban front lines was, not surprisingly, unwilling to give up its power.

As a result the AIA was dominated by the Shura-yi Nazar and contained a number of warlords who had been responsible for grave abuses of human rights. The Pashtuns, the largest single ethnic group in Afghanistan, were under-represented and marginalised from the political process.

The Emergency Loya Jirga (ELJ)

In Pashtun tradition, *loya jirgas* (grand assemblies) have been convened at key moments as a way of making, or legitimising, important decisions. The ELJ was thus an important stage in the process of transition to democratic government. In the first round of elections, organised by the UN, local communities nominated representatives, who then gathered in regional centres to select delegates to the ELJ. The process was subject to pressure from local power-holders, in the form of intimidation, the exclusion of women, and in a few cases direct acts of violence. Nevertheless, in the end the elected delegates (numbering in total just over 1000) represented a diverse range across the political, religious, and ethnic spectrums of Afghan society. There were in addition about 550 appointed delegates. Many of those were also selected equitably, filling places reserved for women and representatives of refugee communities, for example. A number, however, especially those added at the last minute, were members of the military factions, who played a significant role in the intimidation that took place at the actual *loya jirga* in Kabul.

Despite the problems experienced in the selection process, many delegates attended the ELJ with great hopes. '*It was*', said one delegate from Mazar, '*like a great light. It was the most democratic thing that has ever happened in this country.*' Under the terms of the Bonn Agreement, the ELJ was charged with three tasks: electing a head of state for the transitional administration; approving proposals for the structure of that administration; and approving the appointments of key personnel. Yet once they arrived in Kabul, delegates were given little opportunity to address the issues before them, and it was clear from early on that many of the decisions would be made behind the scenes.

▼ *A teacher in Panjao district, Bamiyan province. Such people were chosen to represent their communities in the first round of elections to the Emergency Loya Jirga.*

CHRIS JOHNSON/OXFAM GB

The atmosphere inside the great tent in which the ELJ was held was marred by intimidation, particularly as the ministries of Defence and the Interior succeeded, with the acquiescence of the UN, in bringing the much-feared internal intelligence branch – the National Security Directorate, formerly known as KhAD – into the assembly. In addition, procedural confusion and poor chairmanship were exploited by those wanting to manipulate the agenda to suit their own interests. The result was several agenda-less days, chaotic speakers' lists, and delegates frustrated by not knowing what, when, or how they were to decide issues. Thus, although there were some changes between the Interim Authority and the Transitional Authority that succeeded it, and a number of well-qualified, non-factional people joined the administration, a fundamental shift in power did not take place. A major source of dissatisfaction, especially among Pashtuns, was the way in which the former king, Mohammed Zahir, was persuaded not to stand for the office of president but to support the candidacy of Hamid Karzai.

The constitutional process and the CLJ

The Bonn Agreement states that Afghanistan should have a new constitution. A Constitutional Commission was to have been set up within two months of the establishment of the Afghanistan Transitional Authority to draft a document, which would then be debated and approved by a Constitutional *loya jirga* (CLJ), to be convened within 18 months of the establishment of the ATA. The process by which members of the Commission were appointed was far from transparent; the brevity of the consultation period and the lack of public information – at least outside the capital city – led many people to question the validity of the process and to see it as an exercise in control, rather than genuine consultation.

General elections

According to the timetable agreed in Bonn, elections are due to be held by June 2004. However, free and fair elections presuppose a high degree of security, and this is currently not evident in Afghanistan. Moreover, even to register voters in a country such as Afghanistan, let alone to organise the election itself, requires major resources; by mid-2003, little progress had been made: even the initial population count had not been completed, and funds had not been committed to the task.

None of this necessarily means that elections will not go ahead – there will be a number of pressures to ensure that they are held – but elections that are not widely seen as free and fair could prove dangerous, further destabilising the fragile equilibrium between rival factions, with the risk that Afghanistan will plunge back into war. Added to this is the danger inherent in expecting elections alone to bring about change. Experience from recent post-conflict elections elsewhere shows that massive shifts in power due to elections can spur the defeated to turn away from the ballot box and resort again to violence. The electoral process will reinforce the

► Warlord power still rules in many areas of Afghanistan. Weapons abound, and demobilising the militias is a slow process.

▼ Organising national elections in remote areas with poor infrastructure will be no easy task.

transition to peace only if accompanied by measures to demobilise armed militias, establish civilian control over a unified army, create effective judicial systems, reform the public sector, and share power more equitably within government.

The choice of electoral system will be crucial. First-past-the-post systems, which exaggerate the rewards to the winner, are likely to increase conflict, rather than reduce it. Given the factionalised nature of Afghan politics, the primary goal should be to ensure that each group secures a proportion of seats broadly in accordance with the proportion of votes received. In addition, most Afghans want an opportunity to vote for candidates from their own area, and their distrust of political parties means that voters should be given the chance to vote for individuals as well as for parties. Widespread illiteracy and innumeracy mean that the voting procedure must be simple and transparent, and the results must be easily explicable to a population which has no experience of democratic elections. It is also important that elections should not signal a rapid end of international support for Afghanistan, as has been the case in many post-conflict contexts.

Challenges for the future

JENNY MATTHEWS/OXFAM GB

Security

Ask any Afghan what is the most important issue in Afghanistan today, and the reply in every case will be: *security*. Yet in most places warlord power still rules; progress on the creation of a genuinely national army and the disarmament of factional militias remains desperately slow; and new supplies of weapons continue to flow to the various factions.

The exact number of combatants in Afghanistan is not known, but it is estimated that there are currently some 70,000 men in the regular forces and another 100,000 irregular militia members. However, estimates are unreliable, because numbers can be inflated for reasons of prestige, or in a bid to maximise the resources that come with demobilisation programmes. Three broad groups of armed men can be identified: those who belong to the regular forces, with livelihoods dependent on the military establishment; those who are conscripted into regular forces for short periods, thereafter returning to their communities; and those who belong to irregular militias. The lines between all of these and between those who use guns for banditry or other criminal activity are often blurred. In addition, many Afghans own firearms for self-defence.

In the words of one elder in the southern province of Zabul: '*People are afraid. If they attack our families and we are empty-handed, what can we do?*' It is a vicious circle: more guns mean more fear, which means more guns. The only way out is to create an independent force which people can trust. There should be a national army and police force, but they must be genuinely national bodies: neither commanders nor ordinary citizens are likely to give up their arms to someone perceived to be the leader of a rival faction. Currently the Ministry of Defence is dominated by the Shura-yi Nazar, and in July 2003 the disarmament process was once again postponed because Marshall Fahim refused to remove officials belonging to his own party and create a genuinely national and professional ministry. Afghans have said many times that an international presence is needed to support any disarmament process, but the international powers have shown a marked reluctance to act.

Another reason for keeping weapons is that people often have no other form of livelihood. A woman from Mazar explains it very simply: '*They have no jobs. They go to the commander, and he feeds them.*' Successful disarmament depends on the expansion of education and employment opportunities.

Most Afghans believe that the majority of those under arms would be prepared to give up their weapons if conditions were right; indeed, there have been reports of people simply handing over their arms because they are tired of war and want to find another way to live. But, in the main, disarmament programmes have so far collected only old guns, or weapons left behind by the Taliban. Meanwhile, enormous weapons caches uncovered by Coalition forces, including anti-tank guns and rockets as well as firearms, are being turned over to local (non-government) forces working with the Coalition – precisely those groups that should be disarmed most urgently.

Disarmament will be of little use if the guns collected are simply replaced by new weapons. As yet, there appears to be no control on supplies of new arms entering Afghanistan. Moreover, unless there is a national army capable of ensuring security, disarmament of the major regional forces, like those of Ismael Khan in the west, will only create a vacuum into which other forces will move, including those opposed to the current administration. Progress on the creation of a national army and police force, however, crawls along at a snail's pace: so far only 4000 members of the proposed 70,000-strong army have been trained, and the first police-training course began in March 2003 with only 500–600 participants.

Security in Afghanistan, far from improving, is currently deteriorating. Factional fighting continues in many parts of the country; in the south, centre, and east those opposed to the current settlement are launching increasing attacks on international forces and the staff of international organisations. Yet, despite numerous requests by the UN and the ATA, it was not until NATO took over command of the International Security Assistance Force in August 2003, almost two years after the signing of the Bonn Agreement, that any willingness was shown to consider extending the ISAF mandate to areas outside Kabul. The USA set up three Provincial Reconstruction Teams (PRTs) in early 2003, and shortly afterwards the British established a fourth. The teams combine military and civilian personnel, but they lack the resources to deal effectively with security problems, and few people on the ground believe that their extension is the answer. Some 11,500 US-led Coalition forces are also in the country, but they are there to hunt down al-Qa'eda and have no mandate to protect the civilian population and aid workers.

Rebuilding the economy

Rebuilding the economy will be a formidable task. Even before the war, Afghanistan was one of the world's least industrialised countries. Before the mid-1950s there was no attempt at economic planning, but gradually the state began to assume a more active role in economic development, and in 1965 the first of a series of five-year development plans was launched, with the aim of providing basic infrastructure. Investments were made in mining for minerals, and to a lesser extent in manufacturing and large-scale irrigation projects. Later, the emphasis shifted towards industrial development and support for individual farmers to increase production. Electricity was mainly generated by hydro-electric schemes and supplied only to the towns. Natural gas was discovered in 1958, and exploitation began in 1967. Ninety-seven per cent of it was exported to the USSR at below market prices. Many of the minerals present in Afghanistan have never been exploited commercially.

By the time the war against the Soviets began, Afghanistan's manufacturing industry consisted mainly of small-scale enterprises, involved in processing locally produced commodities, the most important being cotton. Only a few large manufacturing units had been established, operating mainly with state subsidies. The civil war between the *mujahedin* groups devastated the public sector, and the remaining industries were running at well below capacity. Industrial equipment and even the fabric of buildings were either destroyed or taken off to Pakistan. The physical infrastructure had also been shattered, with the road network so severely damaged that journeys which once took a few hours now took all day.

▼ *A war-damaged bridge, one of many which must be repaired if the Afghan economy is to revive.*

DIANNA MELROSE/OXFAM GB

MINES

It is early morning, but the sun is already hot as Mohammed Asham and his team start work. Mohammed is from Ghazni province. Once he fought in the *jihad* with the *mujahedin*; now he leads a mine-clearance team. This is difficult and extremely dangerous work, especially in old residential areas like this. It is necessary to walk with extreme care between the lines of red-painted stones that mark the safe path. In the ruins of what was once someone's house, one of the team is methodically sweeping his metal detector across the rubble-strewn ground. In response to a series of bleeps, he is down on the ground, painstakingly clearing away the earth. This time it is just a harmless fragment of metal. But it is not always so: already they have removed nine mines and seven pieces of unexploded ordnance out of this small sector of ground.

Mohammed's team is part of the Mine Action Programme for Afghanistan, the largest civilian de-mining programme in the world, employing more than 7000 staff and currently working in 15 provinces. Fifteen NGOs operate within the programme, including manual mine-clearance teams; a dog-handling team, specialising in detecting plastic mines and other mines with minimal metal content; a clearance team which specialises in clearing former battlefields of unexploded ordnance; and a bomb-disposal team which destroys high-technology ordnance. Since it began work in 1989, the Programme has destroyed more than three million mines and pieces of unexploded ordnance. Yet its task is far from completed. Between five and seven million landmines are still to be cleared, making Afghanistan one of the most heavily mined countries in the world; between 150 and 300 people are killed or injured by them every month.

The Coalition campaign against al-Qa'eda brought new problems. Bombing of ammunition stores scattered fragments randomly over a wide area, while the use of cluster bombs was something of which the teams had no previous experience. The pressure on them was enormous: agencies wanted to deliver aid; refugees and internally displaced people wanted to return home. Money flowed in – funding in 2002 totalled $60m – but, as with many other areas of work, it is long-term funds that are needed: new teams take time to train and to become operational.

Mines were used not only for defensive purposes, but often to harass the local population, weaken the local economy, and depopulate villages. More than 90 per cent of the mined areas in Afghanistan are fields, irrigation canals, and grazing areas, although the devices have also been laid beside roads, and in residential and commercial areas. The nation's economic recovery depends on their removal. The Mine Action Programme briefs local people, teaching them to identify mines and mined areas. Teams visit schools and offices, offer training at border-crossing points to returning refugees, and use radio, drama, posters, and billboards to communicate their messages.

Afghanistan's new government supports the banning of land mines. With a nice sense of timing, it signed the Land Mine Treaty on 11th September 2002, the 126th country to do so. While the treaty is an important statement of intent, putting it into practice will be another matter. The treaty commits the government, among other things, to destroying stockpiles of land mines. No one knows how many there are, and the task will be almost impossible to achieve in the current situation, where many of the mines are almost certainly in the hands of the various militias. Meanwhile there is a new threat: forces opposed to the US-supported Transitional Authority have begun targeting aid workers – including the de-mining teams – and have forced the suspension of work in some areas.

Another problem was that the formal banking system had collapsed, and people relied instead on the informal system, as did international agencies and people sending remittances home from overseas, with wealthy traders acting as substitutes for banks. Money was deposited with a trader in one location, inside Afghanistan or in a neighbouring country, and cash was collected by the appointed person in a different place. The system worked on trust and it operated effectively. It could, however, be used to handle money from the illegal economy, just as easily as it facilitated lawful transactions.

Smuggling

Once government controls began to collapse in the 1980s, Afghanistan's location meant a dramatic increase in smuggling. Goods of all varieties entered – and continue to enter – across the country's unregulated borders, mostly to be smuggled into Pakistan, where high customs tariffs make such trade extremely profitable. The main route runs from the free port of Dubai, through Iran, entering Afghanistan at Islam Qala, near the western city of Herat. Traders also take advantage of the Afghanistan Transit Trade Agreement, which allows goods destined for Afghanistan to enter the port of Karachi free of import duty. They are transported through Pakistan, enter Afghanistan (legally), and are then smuggled back into Pakistan.
The cost to the Pakistani exchequer of lost revenues due to smuggling has been estimated at between 20 billion and 25 billion rupees a year.

Drugs

It was the trade in opium and heroin, however, that most caught Western attention. Opium-poppy cultivation in Afghanistan has been going on for centuries. It is believed that the crop was first introduced into the province of Badakhshan by traders from China for medicinal purposes. The resulting addiction created a market for opium which led to the systematic cultivation of the crop. However, until the *jihad* against the Soviets, cultivation remained confined to a small area of the country. The war radically changed this. Many *mujahedin* groups used profits from the opium trade to finance their war efforts, and the breakdown of government control in rural areas meant that cultivation and trading could spread unhindered. In 1978 only 200 tonnes of opium were produced; in 1999 the UN estimated annual production at 4600 tonnes. Afghanistan had become the largest single source of opium in the world, producing more than three-quarters of the heroin sold in Europe.

Initially the trade grew under the Taliban, but in 2000 they banned opium-poppy cultivation, and UN and US drugs-control officials subsequently confirmed that poppy growing had been effectively eradicated in all areas under their control. As soon as the Taliban were removed from power, poppy growing resumed, and on an enormous scale. Traditionally, Nangahar and Helmand provinces have been the main areas of cultivation, together accounting for about 80 per cent of all production; but in 2002 new areas which had never before grown the plant were sown: in a highly organised campaign, drugs traders came with seeds, technical advice, and cash up-front. For the impoverished farmers in these remote areas, the offer was too good to resist, and by 2003 virtually every household in many districts of Afghanistan's central highlands was growing poppy. Poppy growing had also surged in some of the areas where traditionally it had been grown. Production increased in Badakhshan in 2000 and 2001 in response to the Taliban's prohibition in other areas; it increased again in 2002, and in 2003 it was almost double that of the previous year's record crop. President Karzai has pledged his commitment to stop the cultivation, but his administration's writ does not extend far beyond Kabul, and there is currently little he can do to put his words into action. Attempts to stop people growing poppy, as in early 2002 in Nangahar province, have been quickly reversed by angry farmers. Donors' efforts to pay farmers for pulling up the crop have been equally unsuccessful: new fields were planted simply in order to claim the compensation, and various scams were devised to claim it without destroying the crop.

Scores of thousands of rural families now depend on poppy production to survive, although the big money goes to the traffickers. Farm-gate opium prices have increased significantly in recent years: it was selling at around $400/kilo at harvest time in 2002, and later in the year was fetching as much as $500/kilo. This makes it massively more profitable than any other crop that farmers can grow: families in many districts report earning easily 30 times what they could get from growing wheat. This price, however, is only a tiny fraction of what the product will eventually fetch on the streets of London or New York. Relatively little processing of poppy into heroin was done within Afghanistan until recently, but now there are perhaps 18 heroin-processing factories in Badakhshan alone.

The routes by which opium and heroin are smuggled out of the country vary according to changing opportunities. In recent years, many traders used routes through Tajikistan and north to Moscow, but with the change of government there have been reports of large quantities also moving south to Kabul, from where it is believed to be flown out of the country. The south-west border with Iran is also a favourite route, for although Iran takes drug control seriously and imposes strict penalties, including the death sentence, for smuggling, the sandy wastelands which form its southern border with Afghanistan are virtually impossible to seal.

While there are still Afghans who oppose the cultivation of poppy because they see it as contrary to the teachings of Islam (and even before the Taliban ban there were examples of districts where poppy cultivation had been stopped), effective, nation-wide action against opium production will be impossible unless law and order is restored in the country. Even then it would be extremely difficult: those controlling the drug trade are enmeshed in regional networks whose influence extends far beyond Afghanistan; they are also well embedded into the war economy of Afghanistan, with commanders at all levels benefiting from the trade, from local areas up to the highest levels.

By 1999, Afghanistan was the largest single source of opium in the world, producing more than three-quarters of the heroin sold in Europe.

◄ *Poppy fields in Darayem, Badakhshan province, where in 2003 the yield was almost double that of the previous year's all-time record. There are thought to be 18 heroin-processing factories in the province.*

▲ *A school in Badakshan: no lessons today, because the teacher is outside, working in the poppy fields. The crop fetches as much as $500 per kilo.*

► *Collecting opium resin from the scored head of the poppy*

► *Signs of the times in Kabul, 2003 –*
above: *a mobile phone shop;*
below: *an early-morning traffic jam*

Prospects for recovery

One of the early actions of the Transitional Authority was to try to get control of the money supply. Uncontrolled printing of currency had been a major cause of inflation since the end of the Soviet occupation, and during the 1990s two separate currencies developed: the government Afghani and the northern (Dostum) Afghani. The ATA brought in new notes, launched at 40 to the US dollar; the old ones had traded at more than 40,000. The change to the new system was completed over a period of three months and to date has succeeded in stabilising the currency.

The ATA has appealed for funds for economic reconstruction projects, but so far the response has been slow. Roads have been identified as a priority by President Karzai, but the construction of the Kabul–Qandahar road, funded by the USA, Japan, and Saudi Arabia, has been hampered by poor security and attacks on the de-mining teams. The road is due to be completed by December

SAM HALL/OXFAM GB

2004, but so far there have been many delays and problems. Other main roads have seen similarly little progress. The same is true for other major infrastructural investments, such as water and electricity supply systems. However, Afghanistan has benefited from new technology in telecommunications, with mobile phones dispensing with the need to undertake the massive task of repairing the old landline system. In general, investments, whether of public or private money, have tended to be in ventures offering a quick return: no one wants to bet too much on the future. Moreover, the absence of a proper legal and regulatory framework, and the lack of government capacity at all levels, continue to hamper reconstruction efforts. On the ground the only viable delivery systems are those developed by the aid agencies – which have tended to continue doing the sort of relief and small-scale development work that they have always done. The basic shift in gear that is needed to support proper reconstruction has so far failed to happen.

A key problem for the new administration has been how to control the customs revenues being taken at the country's borders. Islam Qala, on the border between Herat province and Iran, is by far the most important of these. Since the fall of the Taliban, trade has mushroomed, and every day hundreds of trucks, from modern container lorries to old Russian Kamaz trucks loaded with tyres, draw up at this well-organised customs post. Revenues taken each day are estimated to total one million US dollars, but so far little of this, or of the tolls taken at any other of Afghanistan's borders, has reached the central coffers in Kabul. In June 2003 President Karzai issued a challenge: either the regional power holders submitted their customs revenues to central government, or he would resign. The leaders duly came to Kabul and signed an agreement. Yet, while the result was some increase in revenues for the government, it is unlikely that the regional warlords are not continuing to retain substantial monies for themselves.

Kabul – a capital in crisis

In the early morning the streets are full of bicycles, as men pedal to work, with children balanced on the front and wives and sisters on the back. The once-quiet streets are nowadays clogged by 4 x 4 vehicles and taxis. Men in neat uniforms attempt to direct the traffic, but no one obeys the rules, and before long everything has ground to a halt and horns are blaring in frustration.

Once again restaurants have opened, and imported goods flow in. Rents have spiralled, making a few people rich (mostly commanders and expatriate Afghans), and driving many poor families from their homes. The population of the city now exceeds two million, and poverty abounds. So far there has been no serious attempt to rebuild essential infrastructure or develop sustainable industries. The truth is that Kabul is a city in crisis. There is no sewerage system and hardly any clean water. Property disputes abound, and planning controls are non-existent. There is no vision for what the city should become, and no institutions capable of delivering either urban management or urban reconstruction on the scale required. So far, since the return of the uneasy peace, the city is still served only by aid agencies doing what they always did (but more so), and people chasing quick profits. But cities need more than this: they need investment in public goods, and a coherent, planned approach to their problems. Water supply is a prime example. Only 20 per cent of the city's population have access to piped water, and most of them have it for only a couple of hours a day; the rest rely on shallow wells. Over the recent years of drought, these were dug deeper and deeper as the water-table fell. Despite good precipitation in the winter of 2002/3, the increased population and heavy consumption of water by international agencies and their staff are putting massive strains on the system. There is a great danger that the city will simply run out of water, and that groundwater will become seriously contaminated, as unregulated small industries tip out their waste. None of this can be dealt with by small-scale measures, yet the political confidence that is needed to find a durable solution is absent. Instead, inexperienced organisations tinker about on the edges of the problem with small sums of money, achieving little.

Urban planning is a nightmare. Although a master plan was developed for Kabul in 1974, from the early 1990s the capacity of the authority to provide housing or basic services fell virtually to zero. In the absence of planned provision and controls, people built what they could where they could, often on land whose ownership was unclear, or on steep mountainsides where it will be almost impossible to provide services. The problem was compounded by the ever-changing population and by expropriation of property by successive commanders and political regimes.

▲ ▶ *The ornately decorated Friday Mosque in Herat*

Between the seizure of control by the *mujahedin* in 1992 and the arrival of the Taliban in September 1996, Kabul's residents knew little but war: even the limited periods of calm were punctuated by rocket attacks. The city lay in ruins, more than half its buildings destroyed. Everything of value was looted, from the wires for the trolley buses to pipes for water. In the old carpet bazaar, where once dozens of shops each offered hundreds of beautiful carpets, there were only piles of rubble and the occasional jagged remains of a building. Out on the road to the east, the old industrial estate lay abandoned. Few of the city's educated people can forgive the *mujahedin* for the damage that they wrought, for the obliteration of Afghanistan's cultural heritage. Many families moved numerous times, fleeing from the shifting frontlines, finding shelter wherever they could. Many who had education or money left for Pakistan; those who remained survived on minimal incomes, often selling their own household goods in order to survive. Winter was especially hard, as fuel and food ran low and prices rose. Government salaries were – and still are – virtually worthless. The Taliban brought an uneasy peace, but little reconstruction.

Yet this is a city which was once beautiful; many of its inhabitants loved it and spoke of it longingly from their various exiles. And in small corners it is beginning to re-emerge: an old mosque being lovingly restored, a garden planted; children going to school again; musicians playing rare old instruments. Search and you can still find beauty; but it does not easily show itself: the past has been too grim for that.

Restoring Afghanistan's cultural heritage

To preserve and celebrate the country's rich heritage, Kabul Museum was set up in 1919 at Darulaman in the west of the city. But this area of Kabul was to see some of the worst of the fighting; the museum was all but destroyed, and many of its treasures were looted. Now, with international money coming in for its restoration, Masoudi, the museum's director, sits in his office, the sounds of workmen all around him, and tries to put the pieces back together again. His story bears witness to the Afghan people's will to survive.

'Afghanistan has a very ancient history. Here in this museum you could find pieces that were 60,000 years old. We were at the heart of Asia. Many empires have controlled our land; there were many influences, and you can find in our culture some of the finest, most beautiful results. This museum was one of the best in the world; it contained more than 100,000 pieces. Then, between 1992 and 1995, almost everything was looted. Many groups fought for control of this area;

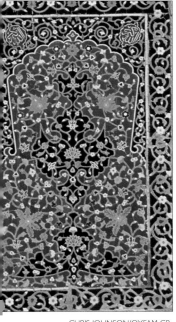

CHRIS JOHNSON/OXFAM GB

they used it as a military base. Our contact with the museum was cut completely, and no one could come here. At the end of 1994, when we could get access again, we planned how to save the remaining objects. With Habitat, the only UN agency still in the city, we bricked up the windows, placed metal doors in front of the old wooden ones, and covered the roof to stop the snow getting in. We started to register the remaining objects, and we moved what we could to safety.'

The courage and ingenuity of those concerned for Afghanistan's cultural heritage meant that they actually saved quite a lot, and when the Taliban took control of Kabul the scholars and curators worked with the new regime to prevent further destruction of the country's treasures. They even obtained letters from Mullah Omar, ordering all provincial authorities to take care of archaeological sites and not to allow illicit traffic in historic objects, nor their destruction. For a time they seemed to be winning. In Bamiyan at the end of 2000, the eager young Talib in charge of culture would tell visitors that Mullah Omar had decreed that Afghanistan's pre-Islamic heritage should be respected. Then came deteriorating relations with the West, and with it the destruction of the Buddhist statues of Bamiyan, and the smashing of many of the objects that remained in the museum.

Now, although foreign money has helped to repair the museum and restore some of its damaged treasures, the resources – both human and financial – for unglamorous but essential tasks such as cataloguing objects and setting up a filing system are still lacking. Meanwhile, at sites throughout the country the pillage of Afghanistan's history still goes on, unscrupulous commanders feeding an equally unscrupulous art market.

CHRIS JOHNSON/OXFAM GB

Music is an integral aspect of Afghan life: everywhere you go, there are musicians. If people cannot afford to buy instruments, they make them from whatever materials are available. The country has boasted many famous singers, female and male. Yet although it was the Taliban who gained notoriety for their attempt to ban music, the restrictions began as far back as 1993, when President Rabbani signed a letter to Radio Afghanistan, forbidding the broadcasting of women singers. During the Taliban years, rolls of ripped-out cassette tape adorned military checkposts, and musicians had their instruments smashed. But you cannot ban a people's culture that easily, and as soon as the checkpoints had been safely left behind, hidden cassettes were brought out, and the music was played again.

Sediq Qiyam *(second right in the photograph)* is an engineer by day, but by night he is one of Afghanistan's best-known musicians. 'Once', he recalls, 'music was a shame, not something that better-class people did. The musicians lived in the Kharabat area of Kabul. They didn't teach their skills to others and they could neither write nor read music. Then, when I was a young man, things began to change. Famous singers came out of well-known families, and the idea that music could be an academic discipline took root.'

Sediq benefited from this change: he learned Western music from an Australian teacher, and the *rubab*, a six-stringed instrument, from an Afghan. He became the youngest player in the Radio Afghanistan orchestra. He went to university to study engineering, and for a while he had no time to practise his music. Then he took up singing. Later he went to India, and used the opportunity to learn more about music. Later still, he obtained an engineering scholarship to study in Poland, where he worked for a PhD. While he was there, he found musicians who had studied in India and he introduced the *rubab* to Polish TV.

Sediq established a factory for disabled people to make musical instruments, but the *mujahedin* looted it. Life was hard in those days, but music kept them going. Fridays were when people relaxed, cooked a meal together, and played music. Then the Taliban arrived. His brother, a journalist with the *Kabul Times* and also a musician, had his instruments smashed. Sediq decided to flee to Peshawar. He stayed there until April 2002; then, full of hope for the future, he came back, wanting to contribute to reconstruction. 'But', he regrets, 'it is impossible: there is too much corruption, and you have to pay a bribe to get almost any contract.' Do people play music again? 'Not like before, because we are afraid. And all of our famous musicians have died or have left this country.'

Land, livelihoods, and environment

Living off the land

Afghanistan's land is as varied as the people who live in it. In the centre and north-east are the high mountain ranges of Hazarajat and the Hindu Kush, mild in the summer and bitterly cold in the winter. To the north are the plains that form the bread-basket of Afghanistan. Parts of the south and south-west are desert.

In 1978, the year before the Soviet invasion, an estimated 85 per cent of the country's 15 million people lived in rural areas, and the country was more than self-sufficient in food. Mountainous regions such as Badakhshan and Hazarajat, however, have always had a food deficit. Even before the conflict with the Soviets, local production in Badakhshan met only half of the province's needs, and at present it meets only one third. Droughts and severe winters compound the problems of poor seed and pest damage. Tractors are little used, and most agricultural work is still done by hand or using animal power. In contrast, the south and north of the country contain

▼ Ploughing for poppy cultivation in Ashtarali, Uruzgan province, 2003. The brothers who own this farm returned from Iran when they heard of the profits to be made from growing poppy.

CHRIS JOHNSON/OXFAM GB

rich agricultural areas, which were centres for commercial agriculture before the Sawr Revolution. Many varieties of fruit-tree were grown, as well as sesame, olives, sunflower, groundnuts, cumin, and grain staples. Qunduz and Helmand were the major cotton-growing areas, and sugar beet was also grown commercially. Rice was an important cash crop.

From the late 1960s onwards, the introduction of mechanisation and chemical fertilisers, together with high-yielding varieties of wheat and rice, led to an increase in agricultural production. By 1975 Afghanistan was reported to be self-sufficient in wheat, and agricultural products were major exports, accounting for nearly 65 per cent of all pre-war export earnings. Lack of water, rather than land, however, continued to be a major constraint on production. The large, modern irrigation schemes designed to improve productivity – such as the Helmand Arghandab scheme – ran into serious technical difficulties, including high levels of salination, as well as social problems caused by attempts to resettle nomadic people.

Cereals were grown on most of the cultivated land, with wheat the principal crop. Livestock rearing was, and remains, a crucial part of the agricultural economy, especially as common grazing rights mean that even landless people can often keep a couple of sheep or goats. Milk products are an important addition to the diet, wool is used to make rugs, and income is earned from the sale of surplus stock.

Increased yields, combined with intricate land-tenure arrangements and a reliance on human and ox power in agricultural production, meant that before the Soviet invasion most people were still able to earn a good part of their living from the land. As a result, Afghanistan did not see the high levels of migration from the countryside that have been common in many countries. Nevertheless,

▼ *Poppy fields, Dai Kundi district, Uruzgan province. The crop was cultivated on this farm for the first time in 2003.*

CHRIS JOHNSON/OXFAM GB

CHRIS JOHNSON/OXFAM GB

▲ *Cows coming home at sunset, Darayem, Badakhshan province. Before the cultivation of opium poppy, there was no road to this village.*

increasing population, combined with inheritance laws which divided land equally between brothers, resulted in many plots being too small to support a family. (In theory, a daughter could also inherit a half-share of land when her father died, but in many cases this did not happen, because on marriage a woman joined her husband's family, and would thus take the land out of the possession of her birth-family.) In areas where tractors were introduced, they deprived poor people of opportunities for earning a living as labourers on others' land. Some of those driven off the land went to work in the cities, but the level of industrialisation was low, and there were relatively few opportunities. Many men went abroad to find work, mostly to Iran and Pakistan.

► *Winnowing wheat, Lal district, Ghor province. Afghanistan was self-sufficient in wheat before the civil war against the Soviet-backed regime.*

Land reform under the Communists

Although limited land reform was attempted under Daoud (1973–78), it was the Communist Khalqi regime which introduced radical reforms to try to dismantle the old feudal relationships. Unfortunately the new authorities understood little of the system that they were trying to change, and their reforms, badly formulated and poorly implemented, made the lives of the peasants worse rather than better. Although inequality certainly existed in Afghanistan, particularly in the northern provinces, it was nowhere near as pronounced as in many parts of Asia. Complex social relationships determined access to land, and in addition to ownership there were various forms of shared rights, for grazing, for fuel collection, and in some areas for rain-fed farming. Traditional systems of reciprocal obligations meant that although landlords might exploit their workers, they also had to look after them.

Most large landholdings were farmed by sharecroppers, who gave a share of their crop to the owner of the land as a form of rent. As tenants were a source of status and political influence, even quite small landholdings which could have been farmed by the owner often had one or more sharecroppers; and, as many plots were very small, their owners also had sharecropping arrangements with larger farms.

To rural people, land was more than just an economic resource: it was integral to their status and identity. As a result, land was more often mortgaged than sold outright, even in situations where the landowner could never hope to regain title to the land. This was true for small farmers, as well as large landowners. The Khalqi decree against this practice abolished the land-use rights of those who had taken mortgages, without giving them any compensation. Most landowners provided seed, and sometimes draft animals; without any alternative way of getting these, people who had been given redistributed land found themselves unable to farm it. The problem was compounded when debts to landlords and money lenders were abolished without providing an alternative form of credit, leaving peasants with no way of obtaining loans. In addition, as large land-holdings were relatively rare, there was not enough land to redistribute. Even worse, the reforms redistributed land without providing for irrigation.

The Russians tried to redress the worst effects of the land-reform legislation, but their presence on Afghan soil unleashed a war that was to wreak even more destruction on agricultural production. From the early 1980s onwards, people fled from the rural areas, especially in the east; the numbers of animals fell drastically, improved seeds and fertilisers became unobtainable, irrigation systems fell into disrepair, many orchards and vineyards were destroyed, and the commercial agriculture sector was virtually eliminated. Production was halved. Yet despite everything, agriculture continued to support people throughout the war years. While there was malnutrition and hunger, there was no mass starvation. Wherever possible, people maintained their agricultural assets, leaving one person behind to look after their trees, even when the community fled. Land ownership tended to revert slowly to pre-reform patterns, though with some new landlords to replace those who had left the countryside, and with new figures in power: the commanders of armed groups.

Drought

Just as Afghanistan was beginning to see some agricultural recovery, it was hit by what many Afghans describe as 'the worst drought in living memory'. It began in the central highlands in 1999, spreading to the whole of the country in 2000 and deepening in 2001.

It is hard to determine how many people were affected. Figures published by the World Food Programme at the beginning of September 2001 suggested that 3.5 million people were in serious need of food aid, although later estimates were much higher. It was, however, clear to anyone who was working in Afghanistan at the time that there was massive crop loss, and in some areas farmers did not even get back the seed that they had planted. Even worse, lack of fodder meant that many people had no way of keeping their animals; the market price of livestock plummeted, and owners were forced to slaughter their stock. It was this, rather than the direct loss of crops, that had the worst effect on poor people's livelihoods. The sale or barter of livestock and livestock products was vital to their economic survival, and their loss meant the destruction of their greatest asset.

The drought affected different parts of the country in different ways. Overall, the worst-affected area was probably the central highlands. Not only did the drought start here a year earlier than in most places, but the area, already one of the poorest in the country, had been blockaded in the previous year by the Taliban in their efforts to subjugate it. While traders had still been able to deliver some grain into the area, taking it at night by donkey over the mountain passes, Hazaras were not able to send their livestock out

CHRIS JOHNSON/OXFAM GB

▲ *Collecting water from a communal tap-stand in Bagh-i Babur, Kabul. Even in cities, piped water is a luxury that few can afford.*

to markets, a fact which led to a collapse in prices. By the time the drought struck, therefore, the poorest people had already lost many of their assets. The drought lasted longer in the south and south-west, and here people suffered terrible losses of livestock. But it was the farmers in the rain-fed northern areas, normally the most productive farming land, who suffered the greatest harvest losses in 2000 and 2001, with many not even reaping what they had sown.

As the drought wore on, it was not only crops that were affected but also access to drinking water. Many Afghans depend on springs or shallow wells, and even in cities access to piped water is a luxury available to very few. By 2000 the semi-desert areas of the south and south-west were badly affected – their problems in places compounded by uncontrolled pumping of water for crops by those wealthy enough to afford such measures. By 2001, even in the mountain areas whole villages were being displaced because they had no access to drinking water. In addition, fruit trees as old as 100 years were dying. The year 2002 saw an improvement in many areas, and the snows in early 2003 were also good. It will, however, take more than one or two years to replenish the water-table, and there is an urgent need for good water management in both urban and rural areas.

Livelihoods

Only the wealthiest of families in Afghanistan can meet all their needs from agriculture: most have to develop a variety of strategies, including cash labour, selling handicrafts, borrowing money, relying on remittances from family members working abroad, and, increasingly over recent years, depending on external assistance. The evidence suggests, not surprisingly, that the drought has affected different families differently. Those who started off with more assets, whether they were settled or nomadic, on the whole managed to keep something and thus retain a base from which to recover. The poor, however, often became heavily indebted and generally lost all their livestock. The drought also affected patterns of land tenure: many of those who left their home area had to mortgage their land in order to raise the money to travel. Now, as internally displaced people (IDPs), living on the margins of the rural economy, many have no way of recovering their land, and thus have lost the one asset that might make their return possible.

The increase in poppy growing has also had an impact on rural livelihoods. While the long-term implications are unclear, in the short term in poor areas such as Hazarajat and Ghor, where it is being grown for the first time, the crop appears to have helped recovery. In the first year most families seem to have grown only what they could tend by using family labour; by the second year, however, many were sowing larger areas of land and paying landless labourers to weed the crop, thus spreading the economic benefits even to those without land. The rates of pay in 2003 were well above the norm for the area – indeed, they were high even by city standards. While for some richer families the cash earned was being used in part to buy luxury items such as television sets, for many families it was being invested in long-term assets, replacing livestock lost in the drought, improving their housing, and diversifying their sources of income.

▶ *Ghor province, 2003: the profits from poppy cultivation have brought electricity to Lal district centre for the first time.*

CHRIS JOHNSON/OXFAM GB

Environment

For many years the district of Keshem in Badakhshan was on the front line between the Taliban and the Northern Alliance: hardly the place where one would expect to find an environmental project. But the vision of one man, Khawrin, once the head of the government's Forestry Department, was stronger than the war. In the valley he created a beautiful garden, a gun-free zone used by the whole community, including an area reserved for women. Up the hillsides that were once bare ran rows of trees. It was, and still is, a haven of peace, a place which reminded you of better times, and showed that you were in a part of the world where public gardens had always been cherished, as an integral part of what it meant to be civilised. People saw what could be done and came from far away to buy the saplings and make their own small patches of green. Nurseries now flourish in many parts of Badakhshan, and tree-planting projects help to stabilise the hillsides by preventing soil erosion.

It is estimated that Afghanistan has lost more than 85 per cent of its hardwood forests, much of it to illegal and uncontrolled logging. Most of the forests of Paktia and Kunar have now gone, their timber smuggled out to Pakistan. Only Nuristan has survived – because there is no road to it. At the same time, because of increasing demand for fuel, the hills are being stripped bare of brushwood. Farmers desperate to grow more food are increasingly forced to cultivate the steep mountainsides. This in turn means that the land has less capacity to absorb water, with consequent increases in flooding. Animal dung is being burned for fuel because there are few trees left to cut, so there is little left to fertilise the land. It is not that farmers fail

▼ *Waras district, Bamiyan province, Hazarajat: saplings have been planted along the river banks, but the hillsides have been stripped of timber, and soil erosion is a serious problem here, as in many places in Afghanistan.*

CHRIS JOHNSON/OXFAM GB

DIANNA MELROSE/OXFAM GB

▲ *A timber yard in Bamiyan, with bare hillsides in the background*

to understand the value of environmental measures: one can see places throughout Afghanistan where saplings have been planted along watercourses to stabilise the banks; but the amount of labour required to undertake serious anti-erosion measures in the mountain areas is beyond the capacity of local communities, and the immediate return to any one village or family is low. Nor is it easy to find ways of improving land fertility: waste food is fed to animals, so there is little to compost, and crop rotation is limited by the small size of landholdings and the low value of other crops, compared with the staple wheat.

The desert areas also suffer. The shifting sand dunes of the west and north were once held down by dense bushes. Now they have all been burned. At Zaranj, in the west of Afghanistan, a wide river was once the border with Iran. Now there are only upturned boats and a customs house half buried in sand. In the town, the wells yield only brackish water, and drinking water has to be purchased from tankers, which pump it up from pits dug into the dry river bed.

Water management remains one of the most pressing environmental issues in Afghanistan, in both the urban and rural areas. The problem has been made worse by uncontrolled drilling. In the midst of the drought, a huge quantity of water was being pumped out of the ground to irrigate crops, or sometimes even to run to waste, while in nearby villages wells ran dry and people had no drinking water. Without regulation, even well-intentioned schemes could only make matters worse.

Restoring services

If Afghanistan's new government is to gain any legitimacy with its people, it will have to re-establish a basic level of service provision, most critically in education and health care. This will not be easy.

Education

Even before the war against the Soviet-backed regime, most of Afghanistan's population were poorly served. Although by the early 1970s schools and colleges were well established for the better-off in towns and cities, educational provision was very limited for the urban poor, along with the rural population (80 per cent of the total). Many village schools remained

▼ *Kabul, 1994: a school which survived against all the odds, held in the ruins of an orphanage*

empty, lacking teachers, textbooks, and other resources. Usually all that was available was a *madrasa*, a religious school — and, since the *mullahs* were often not literate themselves, education commonly consisted only of memorising the Koran. Then, during the conflict with the Soviet-backed regime, many schools were destroyed or damaged, and it is estimated that 85 per cent of all teachers left the country. The result was that by 1988 three-quarters of all Afghan children were not being educated.

As central government authority collapsed in many parts of the country, the responsibility for education passed into the hands of the various *mujahedin* groups, who made sure that religious subjects dominated the curriculum. In some places, some form of alternative schooling was provided by NGOs.

After the fall of the Najibullah regime in 1992, schools in Kabul did not open at all for two years. When they finally re-opened, the lack of resources was daunting: school buildings had been destroyed and their contents looted. Children often had to sit on the floor on bare concrete or on plastic sheets. When the Taliban took the city, girls' schools were closed, and although boys' schools could in theory stay open, the level of provision was very limited, in part because women were no longer allowed to work as teachers. Some NGO-provided schools were able to continue in the country-side, but they often struggled for funding, because many donors confined their grants to 'emergency' work, rather than long-term development.

Provision for girls' education has always varied across different parts of the country. Whereas in Herat 42 per cent of girls were in school before the arrival of the Taliban, in Qandahar there has always been a tradition of strong opposition to non-religious education, especially for women: in 1991 the UN estimated that fewer than 5 per cent of the city's school-age population were receiving any sort of instruction at all, and perhaps none of these were girls. However, not all Pashtun areas are opposed to the education of girls. In the provinces of Khost and Logar, in the south-east of Afghanistan, an NGO runs a long-established home-school programme in the villages. About one-third of the students are girls. When the Taliban tried to close the programme, the local people protested that it was their community, and insisted that the schools should continue.

In the remote rural areas, the lack of opportunities for all, but especially for girls, was most acute, because state provision was concentrated in the urban areas. In many parts of Hazarajat, for example, only 2 per cent of girls were receiving formal education, even before the arrival of the Taliban. Yet as the experience of being a refugee or economic migrant opened people's eyes to the benefits of education, attitudes changed, and in many rural areas there is now a high level of community support for schools. To take again the example of Hazarajat, not only have communities made a substantial contribution to NGO-run programmes, but during the time of the Taliban their elders negotiated with local leaders to maintain provision for girls as well as boys, in some districts even managing to continue running secondary schools for girls.

► *Karte Char, Kabul, 2003: a few of the three million children who responded to the government's 'Back to School' campaign*

Soon after the Bonn Agreement was signed, UNICEF and the Afghan Ministry of Education launched a 'Back to School' campaign. They aimed to get between 1.5 million and 1.7 million children back in school: in fact, three million registered. But this was just a beginning. In the rush to enrol children in school, little attention was paid to what they would do once they got there. Many schools still have no text books; only 22 per cent of all teachers have graduated from teacher-training college, and most of those currently teaching have themselves been educated only to Grade 12, or even less. Many teachers are still not receiving regular salaries; even when they do get paid, it is a pittance. Half the schools in Afghanistan have no safe water supply; more than one third lack adequate sanitation. No one knows how many of those three million children who registered for school are still attending – certainly not all of them. Some level of drop-out was inevitable, given the poor facilities and the high hopes generated by the publicity campaign; yet it is amazing how many still do attend school, and with what enthusiasm.

There is an enormous thirst for education in Afghanistan, but as yet little thought has been given to the question of how to create a system that is interesting and relevant to the diverse needs of Afghanistan's children. Officials in the Ministry of Education tend to think in terms of replicating the system that they had 25 years ago, yet the old system only ever provided for a fraction of Afghanistan's children, and now the population has doubled. International organisations think in terms of universal primary education, but the obstacles are daunting: in the very remote areas, many children live far from the nearest formal school, and the transitional authority simply does not have the resources – of personnel or money – to provide schooling in all the rural areas. Moreover, for the poorest children the need to earn money by herding sheep or working in the fields will always limit their educational opportunities. For many children in rural areas, initiatives like Oxfam's village-based winter schools programme may have to be the answer for many years to come. This programme takes advantage of the fact that during the winter in the mountains there is no work in the fields, and even the poorest children have time to go school. The programme has huge support from the communities, but it is unclear how the teachers' salaries will continue to be paid in the long term.

Primary schooling and secondary education are important, but if Afghanistan is to produce the health workers, teachers, lawyers, accountants, and administrators that it needs, it will also require a tertiary system. Kabul University once had a high reputation, but by the late 1990s it was all but destroyed. As a former professor comments: '*Most of the students now don't know the basics of their subjects, and a degree is only a name. All science laboratories have been destroyed, and there is virtually no technical education, because there are no machines on which to learn. Research stopped after the coming of the* mujahedin. *New professors, appointed to replace those who left, don't have the experience and qualifications of their predecessors.*' Although teachers and students, male and female, have returned to the university with enthusiasm, the task of rebuilding will be massive and has scarcely begun.

KHWAJA HASSAN SCHOOL, SHAMALI

Khwaja Hassan School lies in Istalif district in the Shamali plain. This fertile area, just to the north of Kabul, has been the scene of fierce fighting on more than one occasion during the last two decades. Five years ago every household in this village fled, leaving not just their homes and gardens, but even their carpets and their household appliances. Many of the houses were burned. Most of the displaced people went to Kabul, where they sought shelter with relatives or in the shells of destroyed houses. Now they have come back.

CHRIS JOHNSON/OXFAM GB

'We came last year, once the summer started', Abdul Ghani, the headteacher, explains. 'We could not come in the winter: we had no houses, and it was too cold. At first 87 families came, then day by day there were more. This is the third time we have rebuilt this school. At the time of the Soviets, the *mujahedin* came and destroyed it. It was rebuilt. Then the Taliban destroyed it again.'

Both the building of the school and the on-going support for education came from an NGO which had a policy of encouraging girls' education. Before the contract was signed, they discussed this question with the teachers and parents, and everyone agreed that girls should indeed be able to attend school, although they had never done so in the past. Negotiating the agreement was one thing; making it a reality was another. NGO staff would visit, find no girl pupils, and talk with the teachers. The teachers talked with the parents. This went on for a long time, but in the end the girls came, and it is clear that they are determined to make the most of the opportunity.

Health services

The provision of health services will be another major challenge. Afghanistan has some of the highest maternal, infant, and child mortality rates in the world. For every 100,000 babies born, 1600 women die: a rate more than 200 times that in the UK. In many rural provinces the figures are much, much worse: Badakhshan records 6500 deaths per 100,000 live births, the highest reported figure in the world. Almost 90 per cent of these deaths are considered preventable. Among women of child-bearing age who die, almost half do so from complications in pregnancy and child-birth. And if a woman dies in child-birth, her baby stands only a one in four chance of surviving until its first birthday.

Even before the Soviet occupation, the situation was not good. In 1978 there were only about 1300 doctors and even fewer nurses in the country, and Afghanistan relied on foreign aid for what little health care was available. Coverage was estimated at only 25 per cent of the population, yet this figure masked the true extent of the problem, for health services rarely reached the rural population at all.

▲ A student in an empty laboratory at Kabul University, 1996. All the equipment was looted during the battle for the city.

The system was designed to deliver clinical treatment to urban patients, mostly concentrated in the capital. Even in Kabul it was estimated that 30 per cent of those suffering ill health received no medical care at all.

The war brought about an exodus of trained personnel and large-scale destruction of physical facilities. Many health centres fell under the control of commanders or political groups; preventative health care, except occasional vaccination programmes, was non-existent. Where health centres did function, they were staffed by poorly trained workers who concentrated on dispensing drugs.

During the Soviet era, in order to fill the gap in services, communities selected people to attend paramedic training courses, run by a variety of organisations over the border in Pakistan. The courses differed greatly in length, syllabus, and quality, but graduates returned home, hung out their signs claiming to be fully fledged doctors, and encouraged the notion that health care consisted of tablets and injections. Most Afghans believe that the best doctor is the one who gives the most medicines. It is common to see someone returning from the doctor with four or five bags of different tablets; and patients of Western-trained doctors working for NGOs often complain that they were only given one sort of tablet, or did not receive an injection. To make matters worse, many medicines, smuggled and of dubious quality, are freely on sale in bazaars.

Given that Afghanistan lacks not only health services but also the basic necessities for health — clean water, sanitation, and adequate food — it is perhaps not surprising that fewer than 75 per cent of children survive to the age of five. Infectious diseases, particularly water-borne diseases, have reached epidemic proportions in most parts of the country. Although severe malnutrition has so far been relatively uncommon, chronic low-level malnutrition, which weakens resistance to infection, is almost endemic. Poor female health and excessive pregnancies (contraceptive services are rarely available) result in under-weight babies; unhygienic practices, coupled with a lack of vaccination, lead to tetanus. As a result, many new-born babies die. The common childhood diseases are rampant, and whole families of children can be wiped out in an epidemic of measles or whooping-cough. The dramatic and widespread increase in cases of malaria is due partly to the breakdown of the controls which used to limit its spread: once farmers were not allowed to plant rice close to the cities, but now they

▼ *Polio-prevention treatment for refugee children, Pul-i Charkhi transit centre*

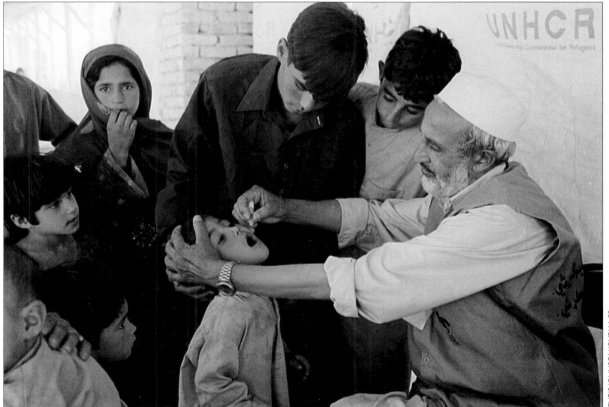

CHRIS JOHNSON/OXFAM GB

plant anywhere, providing the standing water which is a breeding ground for malaria-carrying mosquitoes. Poverty and general ill health have led to a rise in tuberculosis, which is made worse by a lack of information: patients take only part of the course of treatment and stop as soon as they feel better, because they cannot afford to continue to buy the medicine and they do not understand why continuing treatment is important. Drug-resistant strains of TB are developing as a result.

Long-term insecurity, economic stress, and fear for the future have led to an increase in mental illness. Trapped in their homes with the burden of caring for children and sick and disabled family members, it is women who suffer most. Often there is little that a doctor can do: the problem cannot be cured by medical treatment, but by a peaceful settlement of Afghanistan's problems, and by the economic recovery that could bring some hope of employment.

Since the Bonn Agreement, the UN and NGOs have been working with the Ministry of Public Health (MoPH) to rebuild the health system. The task is enormous: health programmes are fragmented between a myriad of service providers, standardisation is rare, and skilled personnel are few. Difficult decisions must be made about what to provide, how much, and for whom. Much of the country's population lives in scattered

settlements in the rural areas. In many places the distance to the nearest clinic is measured not in hours but in days of walking. This means that the provision of health care for these areas will require a combination of community-based services and referral to more central facilities.

Yet despite all the difficulties, there is room for hope. Since the Bonn Agreement, a widespread campaign has ensured that most children are now vaccinated against measles, once a major childhood killer. And although there are few statistics to prove it, those who have worked in remote areas over a long period report that health in general has improved. There is, they say, a combination of reasons for this: water supply and sanitation provision are slowly improving; people have learned new things from health-education programmes, and from their time as refugees in Iran and Pakistan; better roads – thanks to cash-for-work and food-for-work drought-relief programmes – have led to better transport, and this in turn has opened up for more people the possibility of travelling to a clinic.

JENNY MATTHEWS/OXFAM GB

A NEW APPROACH TO PUBLIC HEALTH

Feroza and Khadija (not their real names) work for the Ministry of Public Health (MoPH). But theirs is no ordinary job, at least not in Afghanistan. Rather they are part of a brave attempt to re-think the way in which the Ministry works.

The MoPH in Afghanistan, as in so many countries, has traditionally been dominated by the curative services. Resources were allocated mostly to hospitals. Yet it is well known that the greatest benefits to individual health come through improvements in public health standards, through better water, sanitation, and nutrition. This is where Feroza and Khadija fit in: they work in the new Department of Nutrition. It is not only a new department, but a new way of working, which understands nutrition not merely in terms of Vitamin A and breastfeeding, but as a matter of strengthening women's position in society and supporting households, food security, and social networks. The MoPH works with other ministries, for instance by collaborating with the Ministry of Trade to ensure that salt is iodised – a simple way of preventing iodine deficiency, a major health problem in Afghanistan. It also works in partnership with NGOs, because the MoPH simply does not have the resources to act alone.

The programme is supported by UNICEF and Tufts University in the United States. From the beginning there has been a commitment to developing the capacity of the ministry. This is no mean task in a country which never employed a single nutritionist until recently. Eventually two Afghans were found: one had left 27 years ago to study in the USA; the other, now an Afghan Canadian, left in 1981. They have returned on a temporary basis to work with the ministry.

JENNY MATTHEWS/OXFAM GB

But Afghanistan's health-care standards cannot be improved simply by training. There is the unresolved problem of the underpaid civil service: people cannot be expected to work for $40 a month. UNICEF are therefore paying a 'support salary' of $300, not a fortune but a reasonable sum – and one which could eventually be paid by the government.

But working as a woman in Afghanistan is hard. Feroza is lucky to have a supportive husband, who is also a doctor; but even so, the family are obliged to live with her parents – for how else will their seven-year-old daughter be looked after when she leaves school at mid-day? And female doctors are poorly respected, for the years of the *mujahedin* and the Taliban have taken their toll on the public perception of women. The MoPH has a better record than most: there are more women working here at all levels than in any other ministry. This is partly because health care was always an acceptable occupation for women, even in the Taliban times, but also because its Minister is General Suheila, one of Afghanistan's top surgeons, and a woman who has earned respect not only for her skills but for the fact that she remained working in her country through the most difficult of times. Her second-in-command is a man of remarkable vision. Not all ministries are so fortunate.

The return of refugees and displaced people

The world's biggest refugee population

Since 1979 more than six million people have fled from Afghanistan, mostly to Iran or Pakistan. Although many have returned, by September 2001 there were still 3.6 million Afghan refugees in the region – the largest single refugee population in the world.

When the initial exodus to Iran took place, there were already 600,000 Afghans working there, attracted by the oil boom. The newcomers used their contacts, settled in towns and villages, integrated with the local population, and filled labour shortages caused by the Iran–Iraq war. Eventually, there were 2.8 million refugees in Iran. Virtually no NGOs were present to support them; UNHCR provided some assistance, but otherwise the government of Iran took responsibility for the refugees. Until 1992, refugee status was granted to all Afghans arriving in Iran; when the policy was discontinued, a large group of Afghans were considered by the Iranian authorities to be illegal migrants. Refugees began to return to Afghanistan in 1992, and since then more than one million have moved back. Most returned reluctantly, under pressure from the Iranian government. Life in Iran was markedly better than in Afghanistan, and people had become accustomed to an urban lifestyle, health services, schools for their sons and daughters, a choice of food in the shops. And as one Afghan working in Iran in the early 1990s could easily support a whole family back in Afghanistan, there were strong economic incentives to stay.

Pakistan gave asylum to even more Afghan refugees than Iran did, though with far more international assistance. At its peak, in 1989, the Afghan refugee population in Pakistan was 3.3 million. Most of the early refugees were Pashtuns from the eastern provinces, who crossed the border to Pakistan's North West Frontier Province (NWFP). Others, mainly from the south, went to Baluchistan. They had considerable freedom of movement, and many travelled farther afield in search of work, often leaving families behind in the camps. Some found work in the towns, others in the Gulf countries and Saudi Arabia. There was also migration back across the Afghanistan border on a seasonal basis, a pattern which had existed since long before the war against the Soviet occupation.

► *Refugees collecting plastic sheeting from an emergency distribution point, 1996*

SUE EMMOTT / OXFAM GB

The refugee population in Pakistan served as a military base during the war, and for the political organisation of the resistance parties. In order to qualify for rations, refugees had to join one of these parties. Traditional social structures were undermined, as food rations turned refugees into dependants and weakened their own systems of mutual obligations. The administrative structure of the camps, which worked through heads of families rather than through village representatives, also increased individualism and social fragmentation.

The first wave of refugee return began after the Soviet withdrawal in 1989; it continued in greater numbers after the fall of Najibullah in 1992. At the same time, the violence in Kabul began to give rise to a new exodus, including many educated people, such as teachers and university professors. They were rarely able to get good jobs in Pakistan, and were disliked by established refugees because they were seen as 'communists'. For the women among them, the restrictions of the conservative society of NWFP were new and unwelcome.

By the mid-1990s, attitudes towards Afghan refugees were hardening in both Pakistan and Iran, while deteriorating economic conditions made it more difficult for refugees to earn a living. In Iran there were periodic round-ups of Afghans, including those who had legitimate papers; people were taken to detention centres, from where they were deported back to Afghanistan. In an attempt to regularise the situation, UNHCR in 2000 agreed with the Iranian authorities a programme by which those coming forward for registration were offered an assisted repatriation package if they could not demonstrate their continued need for protection. By the end of the year more than 130,000 Afghans had returned under this programme, and a further 80,000 had obtained permits to remain in Iran for the next 12 months.

In Pakistan, Afghans also faced increasing harassment, even when they had documentation proving that they were eligible to stay. Support from international donors was dwindling, and there was an increasing conviction that the Afghans were not suffering persecution but were economic migrants fleeing from the drought. From January 2000, Afghans arriving in Pakistan were no longer considered refugees, and from November of that year Pakistan officially closed its border with Afghanistan. Although it was impossible to stop people crossing, either by unofficial routes or by bribing the border guards, this move did send out a strong signal that Afghans were no longer welcome.

Internal displacement

In addition to the refugees who sought refuge outside the country, some two to three million people have been driven from their homes by armed conflict but have remained within the borders of Afghanistan. Displacement has occurred both between and within cities, and to and from the rural areas; the composition of the urban areas has changed as a result. The fighting in Kabul in the early 1990s forced many families to move several times. A survey in Kabul's District 3 in 1996 showed that more than half of those interviewed had lived in their current house for one year or less – and a quarter of them for six months or less.

The drought too caused people to leave their homes. At first it was mainly individuals seeking work to support families back home; but, as the drought bit deeper, and especially when drinking water also dried up, whole families were found on the move. Many lost all their assets and have no way of returning.

▼ *Returning from Iran, refugee children wait for onward transport from Gozargah transit centre in Herat, 2003*

The fate of refugees since 11th September 2001

Following the attacks in the USA by al-Qa'eda in September 2001, the security problems created by the Coalition campaign against terrorism, combined with fears about winter-time food supplies to the mountain areas, led to further displacement in Afghanistan. The numbers of people seeking to cross the border were, however, nothing like the one million that had been predicted by UNHCR. Pakistan and Iran kept their borders firmly closed throughout the conflict, with the compliance of the international community, apparently out of concern to prevent the

▲ *Waiting for transport at the UNHCR transit centre at Pul-i Charkhi, Kabul, 2003. But what will refugees find when they return home?*

movement of al-Qa'eda and Taliban personnel. Most senior figures, however, had escaped across the border early on in the conflict, and any who remained were hardly likely to cross at official borders in preference to the unofficial routes across the mountains.

At the border-crossing points, would-be refugees lived in squalor, without food, water, or latrines, setting up makeshift camps in the desolate no-man's land between two countries. Those who found ways across told reporters how they had to resort to dangerous unofficial routes into Pakistan, and how they were beaten at unofficial checkpoints when they could not afford to pay big bribes. Even those who had valid visas faced problems getting in to Pakistan. This problem hampered the humanitarian assistance effort, because Afghan staff of relief agencies were reluctant to cross from Pakistan to Afghanistan for fear that they would not be able to return to their families in Peshawar and Islamabad.

The camps presented the UN with a dilemma. Caught between managing them (and thus undermining the case for asylum) and leaving people with neither food nor facilities, the UN compromised: the World Food Programme provided food, and UNHCR supplied non-food items, both for camps inside Afghanistan and for those in the 'no man's land' between Afghanistan and its neighbours. The lack of security, however, posed serious risks to the would-be refugees and made it difficult for aid agencies to operate. Despite closed borders, Pakistan was estimated to have hosted more than 70,000 refugees in camps in Baluchistan and NWFP, and Iran was estimated to have received around 60,000 new arrivals.

Scratching a living in the market, Kabul, 2003: life is so hard in Afghanistan that many returned refugees have gone back to Pakistan

CHRIS JOHNSON/OXFAM GB

Coming home

The change of government led to the largest and most rapid return of Afghan refugees ever seen, and to the largest UNHCR-assisted repatriation programme anywhere in the last 30 years. UNHCR had estimated that 400,000 refugees would return from Pakistan in 2002, and a similar number from Iran. Yet by October 2002 the UN had assisted more than 1.7 million to return, 1.5 million of these from Pakistan. The return was proclaimed a success, by both UNHCR and the Transitional Authority, yet the reality was rather more complex. Firstly, the figure, although an accurate reflection of those who received assistance, is not an accurate record of those who actually stayed in Afghanistan. A number of families collected assistance, sometimes on multiple occasions, even though they had no intention of settling in Afghanistan. Many made the journey with a genuine intention to stay, but when they arrived they found life so difficult that they decided to return to Pakistan.

Afghanistan was deeply impoverished by the years of war and the drought, and in many places security was poor; outside Kabul the state was barely functioning, and there were almost no programmes to support the kind of development that would make return sustainable. In such circumstances, it is less surprising that returnees went back to Pakistan than that they travelled to Afghanistan in the first place. Certainly there was a push factor – life in Pakistan was not easy for many Afghans – but the crucial pull factor was the strong message that Afghanistan was being rebuilt, that this would be an exciting time of opportunity. This message came in many forms, from the international media broadcasts about reconstruction, to the state propaganda of host countries wanting to see the back of their refugee populations. As one returnee noted: '*All the world was telling us they were rebuilding Afghanistan*'. For many, the disappointment was bitter when they arrived back in their home areas to find little or no support to rebuild their lives.

A typical story is that of Barat Ali, encountered in Gozargah Transit Centre in Herat, the place where returnees from Iran are 'processed': here they collect their cash entitlements and food rations, get their vaccinations, and find transport to their destination. Barat Ali was a tailor, although now his eyesight is too poor and his sons must care for him. He left Afghanistan 23 years ago, when the Russians first came, because he did not want his sons to do military service. The family made their way to a small town in the west of Iran, where he did his tailoring and his sons ran a bakery. They worked hard and managed OK and yet, he said, '*the Iranians did not see us as their people*'. Recently things had got worse: there were hard words about Afghans, and the pull of the 'home country' seemed strong. They decided to return. At first they wanted to go to Kabul, but they no longer had their house; when they heard tales of how hard it was to find accommodation, they decided to go instead to Mazar, where at least they have relatives. They face an unknown future, but two sons remain in Iran, and the one returning home with Barat Ali has a diploma in Human Sciences, so at least he has hopes of finding a job.

Palawasha and her two sisters have a different story. They left Kabul in the early 1990s, when they were still in their teens, '*because our honour was in danger*'. With their father and mother, they travelled for three days and three nights until they finally reached Karachi, where they had relatives. '*It was terrible: there was no work, and it was so hot. But they were nice people, they were kind to us.*' Asked why they had decided to return, Palawasha replied: '*We heard that there was a government. Every day our eyes were to the news. We hope lots from the new government, we want to see our people free. We want to take our house back.*' It will not be easy: the current court system is both corrupt and notoriously slow, and many families have struggled for years to reclaim their homes.

▼ *Pul-i Charkhi transit camp: one of a fleet of brilliantly painted trucks, bringing refugees back from Pakistan*

▲ *Mohammed Khan at Shaidayee camp for internally displaced people, 2003. Contemplating the thought of return to his village, he asks:* 'Shall I eat dust?'

The authorities have expressed their desire to see internally displaced people (IDPs) return to their places of origin wherever possible, and they have made plans to close a number of IDP camps. In some ways it is understandable: many of these people have been displaced for a long time, and the cause of their original movement has long since blurred into the general poverty and uncertainty that is Afghanistan. Yet most do not want to go back. At Shaidayee IDP camp on the outskirts of Herat, one of those that the authorities plan to close, it was hard to find any displaced people who were interested in returning to their original home. Most had been forced to leave by a combination of fighting, poverty, and, in latter years, drought. Barhuddin was typical. He left his home at Taiwara, in the province of Ghor, nine years ago.

'*There was tribal conflict and factional fighting. We were the poorest people. We had no guns, and we were forced to give money to the commanders: first one side, then the other. We were ill treated, some were tortured. We all left at the same time, 400 families, and travelled with our donkeys. I stayed here in Herat for some while, then I went to Iran. Two years ago I left Iran, because there was no employment and I could not pay the rent on my house. I came back to Afghanistan, to Shaidayee. Here at least I can get some work in the town. We used to receive assistance here, but now we get nothing. But I will not go back to Taiwara. The memories are too bad. I do not want any news of there, I just close my eyes. If this camp shuts, I will look for somewhere else to stay; if necessary I will even go to Pakistan. I will not go home.*'

Barhuddin's friend Mohammed Khan came from Ghomarch district in Badghis province. He too was not going back. '*Shall I eat dust?*' he asked. Unlike Barhuddin, he had left his home only eight months ago, driven out by a mixture of conflict and drought. He is landless, although he used to have animals: two cows and 20 sheep. '*When we had animals it was easy, but when you do not have animals, how can you survive? We just try to find a place to live until we die.*'

Even those who wanted to go back said that they could not. Some had mortgaged their land to raise money for the journey and now, scratching a bare living on the margins of the urban economy, had no way of redeeming it. Others simply said that the insecurity in their old home was still too bad.

Justice and human rights

In the past one hundred years three different legal systems have operated in Afghanistan, often simultaneously. These are 'traditional' local codes, the best developed of which is the *Pashtunwali* (the Pashtun code); the *Sharia* (Islamic law); and modern state law, derived partly from the West and partly from other modernising Muslim countries.

Until the late nineteenth century the role of the state in judicial affairs was limited, and outside the towns the settlement of disputes relied on local customary law. Thereafter, Afghan rulers tried to establish either state law or *Sharia*, and attempted to gain control over the interpretation of the latter in order to present their rule as legitimised by Islam. The constitution of 1923 established the concepts of universal citizenship and human rights, and for the first time made the king subject to the rule of law. The balance of religious and secular power shifted back and forth as regimes changed, but it was not until 1964 that the judiciary was granted independence from the state. A Supreme Court was established, and an attempt was made to set up a uniform system of courts throughout the country. Although the plan was never fully realised, Afghanistan's record on human rights improved noticeably between 1963 and 1973.

After 1973 the situation worsened; following the Communist *coup* in 1978, repression and violations of human rights rose to a hitherto unprecedented level. The number of victims who died in the period between the *coup* and the Soviet invasion will probably never be known, but it has been estimated at between 50,000 and 100,000. There was a brief respite immediately after the Soviet invasion, as the new government tried to gain legitimacy. An amnesty for political prisoners was declared, but further waves of arrests soon started. During the ten years up to the signing of the Geneva Accords in 1988, an estimated 1.24 million Afghans lost their lives. Mostly this was due to indiscriminate bombardment of villages, but tens of thousands also 'disappeared' after being arrested; there were summary executions, and massacres in the countryside. People who were suspected of anti-government views were detained without trial, and torture was widely used.

After the Soviet withdrawal in 1989, the regime introduced limited reforms, but violations of human rights, including torture and execution of captured *mujahedin*, still went on, though on a reduced scale. Militias operating in alliance with the government continued to commit abuses against civilians, looting their property and extorting money; prisoners of war were executed. The resistance groups were equally culpable: they kidnapped, imprisoned, and killed those whom they considered rivals, both within Afghanistan and in Pakistan. The indiscriminate use of notoriously inaccurate rockets also caused many civilian casualties. Such abuses were rarely condemned in the West, and indeed some of those receiving the greatest support from the West were the worst offenders. It appeared that the human rights of Afghan civilians counted for little, compared with the body count against the Soviets.

After the *mujahedin* take-over in 1992, the lack of centralised authority in large parts of the country and widespread factional fighting created a situation described by Amnesty International as one where human-rights abuses were committed with impunity and the rule of law was virtually absent. Extortion and kidnapping became commonplace, and all parties to the conflict engaged in the torture and execution of prisoners. Many women were raped, being targeted as the wives, sisters, or mothers of men regarded as enemies by one or another armed group. Educated women in particular suffered, as they were accused of having violated Islamic norms of behaviour.

▼ *Medical students at the University of Kabul, 1996. Before the Taliban arrived, the proportion of women students was high.*

JENNY MATTHEWS/OXFAM GB

This lawlessness was a major reason why initially the Taliban received widespread support. Yet in their relentless pursuit of control, they too showed little regard for the rights of others. Their rocket attacks on Kabul killed and maimed civilians. As their drive to take over the country met with increasing resistance, so too the level of human-rights abuses increased. Punishments for crime included amputation of limbs, flogging, and sometimes even stoning to death.

Women's rights

The years of war have extracted a terrible toll on women's rights. In the past, women could rule an empire, and in the 1970s they were Cabinet ministers and active in every sector of the economy; but when the Taliban took control, women were no longer allowed to work outside the home, nor their daughters to attend school. However, the Taliban's edicts were not the first restrictions on women's rights: under Rabbani's presidency, women were ordered to stay at home and modify their behaviour. The *mujahedin* perpetuated the repression. Even in the north-eastern city of Faizabad, which was never

JENNY MATTHEWS/OXFAM GB

▲ *A glimpse of white shoes – forbidden during the Taliban years – under a burqa.*

controlled by the Taliban, women did not feel able to go out without wearing the *burqa*; those who were employed by NGOs and the UN often did not feel safe to travel to their offices, but worked instead from their homes. It was the repression by the Taliban, however, which was the most systematic.

Women did not take to the restrictions easily. When the Taliban closed the public bathhouses in Herat, 150 women demonstrated in protest. Twenty of them were arrested and imprisoned. The following day all the shops closed in a display of solidarity. In Kabul, resistance was more private, perhaps because the terrible fighting of 1992–1994 had caused so much displacement that there was little social cohesion left in the city. Yet women still found their own ways to resist: from under the *burqa* peeped out the high-heeled shoe, the fishnet tights, the painted toenails. The letter of the law was kept, but the spirit of the law was broken. Desperation as well as defiance drove women to ignore the regulations. They sneaked out to do jobs as domestic workers, because they could not afford to lose the wages; or worked from home because they could not go to the office. But they ran great risks.

Western development agencies that protested about the Taliban's attitudes to women faced righteous indignation. Where, asked the Taliban, was the West when the *mujahedin* raped, kidnapped, and killed women? The charge had no answer, for the West, using the *mujahedin* for its own ends, had ignored the plight of women. The Taliban claimed that once they had control over the whole country and security had improved, they would then introduce proper Islamic conditions, and women would be able to work and study once more. But they never did control the whole country, and the rules got more, not less, restrictive. Attitudes began to change too, with men forbidding their wives and daughters to leave the house, fearing the consequences of flouting the Taliban edicts: '*In seven months*', said one Kabuli grandfather, speaking in early 1997, '*we have gone back 70 years.*' But although the Taliban's version of Islam was an affront to educated women of the cities, for many rural women it made little difference, particularly in the Pashtun provinces. Here, women have always been subject to the restrictions imposed by a tribal society and its centuries-old code of honour. Yet, as in all rural areas, they make a vital contribution to the economy of home and village. And although they are segregated from political and social decisions beyond the walls of their homes, they still have informal influence.

It will take a long time to regain the ground that has been lost, let alone to move forward on women's rights. In the months after the fall of the Taliban, few women could be seen on the streets without a *burqa*, even in Kabul. When asked why by Western journalists, their reply was simple: '*We do not feel safe*'.

▲ *Kabul street scene, 2001*

And although the return of women to jobs and education, together with the creation of a Ministry of Women's Affairs, and the influx of substantial donor funding for programmes with women all make it seem as if a new day is dawning, the reality is less promising than this suggests. So far there is no coherent policy concerning women's rights, in either the donor community or the Karzai government. Without this, it is likely that projects will remain marginal, and at best symbolic. Many of the restrictions that hit the headlines at the time of the Taliban are still in operation. For example, the Taliban's insistence on women being accompanied by a *mahram*, a male relative, whenever they travelled away from home was not just something dreamed up in the 1990s: for many Afghans it is part of their cultural practice. Just because it is no longer a rule does not mean that it has disappeared as a problem. Even for women from relatively liberal families, the question of where they will stay at night when they are travelling for work is, in a society where public space is still dominated overwhelmingly by men, a very real question. So also is the problem of security. And provision for child-care. Until significant progress is made on tackling these issues, the improvement in women's rights will remain more theoretical than real.

A new beginning?

With the Bonn Agreement came a commitment to tackle the serious difficulties that beset the formal system of justice in Afghanistan. The transitional arrangements include the establishment of a Judicial Commission, whose tasks include clarifying, and where necessary reforming, the legal codes of Afghanistan, and the creation of an Afghan Independent Human Rights Commission.

The task is huge. Many courts lack the most basic facilities, and legal appointments have often been made for political reasons, resulting in an ill-qualified judiciary. There is frequently little interaction between the various components of the system – the Supreme Court, the Ministry of Justice, the police, and the prison service. Corrective regimes or rehabilitative programmes do not exist, and there is currently little appropriate provision for women, or for juveniles of either sex.

Given the lack of resources to operate the formal system, and the corruption frequently encountered, it will be necessary to take account of traditional mechanisms of justice and to link them into the formal system. These systems are at their most comprehensive in the traditional Pashtun tribal areas, but they exist to some degree throughout the country. Disputes are resolved through a process of mediation and reconciliation between the parties, which commonly involves seeking forgiveness and pardon, and the obligatory acceptance of a truce. Many Afghans prefer this system to formal judicial institutions, because the process is conducted by respected elders, and decisions are reached in accordance with accepted traditions and values. Also, unlike in the state courts, disputes are settled without long delays and without financial costs. Another problem is that illiteracy discourages people from using formal courts: the overwhelming majority of Afghans are unable to make applications, because they cannot read or understand the laws, and cannot do the proper paperwork. Furthermore, while the state justice system criminalises and excludes convicted offenders, the traditional system generally aims to reconcile disputants and reintegrate offenders into the community. Yet traditional systems also have their problems. The over-riding principle is the good of the community, not the needs or interests of the individual. This is particularly evident in relation to women, whose rights are often denied in settlements. But progress is possible even here, as can be seen from the comment of an elder in Zabul who, explaining why in his area girls were no longer given in marriage as part of dispute settlements, said: *'We learned it was not in accordance with Islam, and the Shari'a must be obeyed.'* The crucial issue will be: who in Afghanistan has the authority to determine the interpretation of Islam?

▼ *Many Afghans have more faith in traditional systems of justice, administered by local elders, than in the state system.*

JENNY MATTHEWS/OXFAM GB

The Afghan Independent Human Rights Commission

The Afghan Independent Human Rights Commission, established by the Bonn Agreement, is the lead agency for human-rights issues in Afghanistan. It has a head office in Kabul and regional offices in the provinces. Its work includes developing a national plan of action for human rights in Afghanistan; monitoring and investigating violations; undertaking a nation-wide consultation on the difficult issue of transitional justice and addressing the abuses of the past; providing human-rights education; and promoting the rights of women and children. Initially set up under the Bonn Agreement for the life of the transitional authority, the commission is planned to be established as a permanent body, whose role is written into the Constitution.

Some extremely brave and committed Afghans have joined the Human Rights Commission, and their record of work throughout the years of war has been exemplary. Yet, in a country where warlord power still holds sway, their task is extraordinarily difficult. To make any real progress in such a situation requires a high level of international support for their work and for their political protection. This has not, as yet, been forthcoming. The pressure to maintain short-term stability has meant that the UN and its international backers have been wary of taking a strong stand on human rights. Many Afghans, however, feel that there must be some accounting for the past, and that without it no lasting peace will be possible. In the words of Dr Sima Samar, the Chair of the Commission: '*We cannot have proper peace without justice. Yet we cannot start justice from today. If we do not tackle things, it is like we do not remove the landmine, we just put another shovel of earth on it – and you know what then happens. We must start talking about justice to lay the foundation for the future. We cannot close our eyes. We cannot just allow a general amnesty. At least these people should ask forgiveness, to accept the truth. At least we should have this.*'

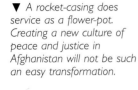

▼ *A rocket-casing does service as a flower-pot. Creating a new culture of peace and justice in Afghanistan will not be such an easy transformation.*

NAC
ENVIRONMET

In conclusion

▲ *What lies ahead for Afghan refugees returning to their war-ravaged country?*

So far a fragile peace has been maintained in most of Afghanistan, yet by the end of 2003 the writ of the Karzai government still did not extend far beyond Kabul, factional politics remained as complicated as ever, and security was deteriorating. The continuing struggles for power of the various groups who are formally party to the Bonn settlement have created pockets of fighting in many parts of the country, and their rivalries have, as so often in the past, been aided and abetted by various regional powers. Meanwhile those who are opposed to the government have gained ground, organising opposition from bases in Pakistan and Saudi Arabia. It is not surprising, therefore, that the primary concern of most Afghans is security. Yet the major powers for a long time refused to support an expansion of the International Security Assistance Force, and little was done to make conditions safer in the provinces.

Politics is almost as much a problem. The narrow base of the Transitional Authority and the past behaviour of some of its key members have compromised its legitimacy among Afghans. Yet without legitimacy it is impossible to govern in the long term. The government needs, therefore, to show the people that it has something to offer them. That it can bring peace, jobs, and some basic services. That it can pay realistic salaries and tackle corruption. So far, all this has yet to happen.

The international presence in the country is something of a double-edged sword. Almost any Afghan will tell you that they want an international presence to remain, that one of the reasons why Afghanistan descended into chaos in the 1990s was that the international powers turned their backs on the plight of the country. Unlike in Iraq, the Americans are still generally welcome here. Yet it is a welcome which could easily be outstayed.

The Coalition's continuing hunt for al-Qa'eda entails unacceptable infringements of the privacy of people's homes, and the killing and wrongful imprisonment of civilians. International personnel, military and civilian, react to their fear of attack by blocking off more and more roads and surrounding their compounds with razor wire. In Kabul in particular, the obtrusive presence of foreigners with their fancy vehicles and their expensive homes and offices raises questions about where all the aid money is going, and whose country this has become. Meanwhile most Afghans see little improvement in their lives. It inevitably leads to resentment.

For all the high hopes and fine words of the recent past, Afghanistan still lacks a true peace settlement. It is in everyone's interest that serious political attention is given to finding one – for the future of Afghanistan will affect us all.

► Dai Kundi district,
Uruzgan province, 2003

CHRIS JOHNSON/OXFAM GB

Facts and figures

(Data are unreliable. The most recent census, in 1978, was aborted before completion.)

Land area
652,000 sq km

Population
Estimated at around 27 million

Capital city
Kabul (population approximately 2.2 million)

Ethnic groups
The main ones are Pashtun, Tajik, Hazara, Uzbek, Turkmen; minor ones include Baluch, Nuristani, Brahui, Qizilbash

Religion
99 per cent Muslim (approx. 80 per cent Sunni, 20 per cent Shi'ite)

Literacy
The UN estimates literacy at less than 10 per cent overall, and probably no more than 2 per cent for women

Languages
Dari (Persian) and Pashto are the official languages; there are more than 30 other languages, of which only Uzbek, Turkmani, Arabic, and Baluchi have written forms

Literacy
UN estimates less than 10 per cent overall, and probably no more than 2 per cent for women

Life expectancy
40 years (UNDP)

Infant mortality
165 per 1000 live births (UNICEF 2002)

Under-5 mortality rate
256 per 1000 live births (UNICEF 2002)

Maternal mortality
1600 per 100,000 live births (UNICEF 2002)

External debt
Estimated at $5 billion in 1990, the bulk of it owed to the Soviet Union. No debt has been serviced since 1992.

Access to safe water
23 per cent of population (World Bank 2003)

Adequate sanitation
12 per cent of population

Electricity
6 per cent of population

CHRIS JOHNSON/OXFAM GB

◄ *Street traders in Kabul, 2003*

Who's who in Afghanistan

Abdullah Abdullah Minister of Foreign Affairs in the AIA and ATA and (with Fahim and Qanooni) one of the powerful triumvirate of Shura-yi Nizar ministers in the new government.

Brahimi, Lakhdar UN envoy to Afghanistan from 1997 to 1999. Returned after the fall of the Taliban as the Secretary General's Special Representative and head of UNAMA (UN Assistance Mission to Afghanistan).

Daoud Cousin of Zahir Shah, Prime Minister 1953–63. Overthrew Zahir Shah in 1973 to become President of Afghanistan. Killed in 1978 *coup*.

Dostum, Abdul Rashid Militia commander during Najibullah's presidency. Mutinied in January 1992 and seized control of the north. Driven out of Mazar by the Taliban. Returned after their fall to become one of the key power-holders in the north. Leader of Jumbish.

Fahim, Mohammad Appointed by Massoud as his successor. Became Minister of Defence in the AIA and ATA and gave himself the title of Marshall. Vice President of the ATA. Widely regarded as the most powerful man in Afghanistan.

Ghani, Ashraf Worked for many years for the World Bank in the USA before returning to be head of the Afghan Assistance Coordination Authority. After the ELJ, he became Minister of Finance in the ATA.

Hafizullah Amin Prime Minister in April 1979; became President in September 1979 after he had Taraki killed. Killed by KGB, December 1979.

Hekmatyar, Gulbuddin Leader of Hizb-i Islami. Prime Minister in the Rabbani government. Now in alliance with the Taliban and other forces opposed to the present settlement.

Jalali, Ali Ahmad Returned from exile in the USA in early 2003 to head the Ministry of Interior. Reportedly charged with ending domination of the ministry by Shura-yi Nizar, he has also been replacing troublesome provincial officials with people loyal to Karzai.

Karmal, Babrak Founder of PDPA, leader of its Parcham faction. Deputy Prime Minister of DRA April 1978, exiled July 1978, returned with Soviet troops. Secretary General of PDPA and President of Revolutionary Council 1980–86. Exiled to USSR.

Karzai, Hamid Pashtun from Qandahar, Chairman of the AIA and the ATA, and current President of Afghanistan.

Khalili, Karim Hazara, leader of Hizb-i Wahdat, a Vice-President in the ATA.

Ismael Khan Co-leader of Herat mutiny, March 1979. Member of Herat *shura* (council) from April 1992 until September 1995, when he was driven out by the Taliban. Fled to Iran. Spent several years in gaol in Qandahar during the Taliban era. Now back as the Governor of Herat. Member of Jamiat-i Islami.

Malik, Abdul Uzbek commander, formerly loyal to Dostum. Allied with the Taliban to take control of Mazar-i Sharif in May 1997, then turned against them. Driven out of Mazar in September 1997.

Massoud, Ahmad Shah Led the *mujahidin* resistance in Panjshir Valley. Founded Shura-yi Nizar (Supervisory Council of North), a grouping of Jamiat commanders, in 1985. Defence Minister for ISA (Islamic State of Afghanistan). Killed in the Panjshir by a suicide bomber in September 2001.

Najibullah Student leader of Parcham faction. Director General of KhAD (secret police) 1980–85. President of Republic of Afghanistan 1987–92. Resigned in April 1992 and took refuge in UN offices in Kabul. Killed when Taliban entered Kabul, September 1996.

Mullah Mohammed Omar Taliban leader, formerly based in Qandahar, now believed to be in Pakistan.

Qanooni, Yonus Minister of Interior in the AIA, but persuaded to relinquish the position in the ATA in response to complaints about domination of key posts by Shura-yi Nizar. Now Minister of Education.

Rabbani, Burhanuddin Lecturer at Kabul University, and leader of Jamiat-i Islami. Acting President of ISA, June 1992–March 1993; extended his term unilaterally until ejected from Kabul by the Taliban in September 1996.

Sayyaf, Abdul Rasul Pashtun from Kabul Province. Lecturer at Kabul University. Leader of Ittihad-i Islami. Prime Minister of Interim Islamic Government of Afghanistan (IIGA), 1989. A key conservative in the post-Bonn political order.

Taraki, Nur Mohammad Founder of PDPA, leader of Khalq faction. Became President of Revolutionary Council and Prime Minister of the Democratic Republic of Afghanistan in April 1978. Assassinated September 1979.

Zahir Shah Pashtun, educated in France. King of Afghanistan 1933–73, after which he lived in exile in Rome. Returned to inaugurate the ELJ, and now carries the title of 'Father of the Nation'.

► *A checkpoint on the road into the Panjshir Valley, 2003*

CHRIS JOHNSON/OXFAM GB

An Afghan chronology

1839–42 First Anglo-Afghan War

1878–80 Second Anglo-Afghan War

1881–1901 Consolidation of the state under Amir Abdul Rahman

1901 Habibullah succeeds his father

1919 Habibullah assassinated. Amanullah takes throne. Third Anglo-Afghan war

1921 First constitution of Afghanistan

1928 Rebellions against Amanullah. Bacha-y-Saqao proclaimed Amir.

1929 Nadir Shah takes Kabul. Beginning of Durrani dynasty

1933 Nadir Shah assassinated. His son Muhammed Zahir Shah succeeds him.

1949–52 'Liberal Parliament'

1964–73 'New Democracy' years

1973 Ex-Prime Minister Daoud stages *coup*

1978 Sawr Revolution: PDPA takes power

1979 Soviets send in troops

1980 Karmal installed as President of Afghanistan

1985 Gorbachev takes power in USSR. Soviet policy towards Afghanistan begins to change.

1986 Karmal exiled to USSR

CHRIS JOHNSON/OXFAM GB

1987 Najibullah installed as President of Afghanistan

1988 Beginning of Soviet withdrawal

1989 Last of Soviet troops leave Afghanistan

1991 UN tries but fails to achieve a political settlement

1992 *Mujahedin* take Kabul. Under the Peshawar Accords, signed on 26 April, Mujaddidi becomes President, followed by Rabbani. Fierce fighting in Kabul

1993 Fighting in Kabul continues. A new international effort results in March in the Islamabad Accords.

1994 Taliban rescue Pakistani convoy and move on to take Qandahar

1995 Taliban take Herat

1996 Taliban take Kabul. Najibullah executed.

1998 Taliban take Mazar, the last major city controlled by Northern Alliance. US cruise missiles attack sites suspected to be al-Qa'eda training camps, in response to suicide bomb attacks on US embassies in Nairobi and Dar-es-Salaam.

1999 The UN imposes sanctions against Afghanistan. Drought hits the country.

2000 Taliban impose complete ban on poppy growing. Further round of UN sanctions agreed. Drought continues.

2001 Afghanistan enters third year of drought. Massoud assassinated by suicide bombers. US bombers attack Afghanistan in retaliation for September 11th terrorism. Taliban regime falls. Northern Alliance forces walk into Kabul. Signing of Bonn Agreement.

2002 Major donors pledge $4.5bn for reconstruction. Major powers re-open embassies in Kabul. International agencies flock to the city. Emergency *Loya Jirga* held in June. Poppy growing resumes on a massive scale.

2003 New constitution scheduled to be agreed in December by the Constitutional *Loya Jirga*. Lack of security continues to be identified as the major issue facing Afghanistan; warlords continue to hold power, and little progress is made on disarmament.

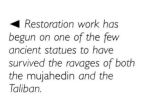

◄ *Restoration work has begun on one of the few ancient statues to have survived the ravages of both the* mujahedin *and the Taliban.*

► *Post-war landscape: a huge outdoor 'salesroom' for used cars and trucks, Herat, 2003*

Sources and further reading

John K. Cooley: *Unholy Wars: Afghanistan, America and International Terrorism*, London: Pluto Press, 2000

Antonio Donini, Norah Niland, and Karin Wermester (eds.): *Nation-Building Unraveled? Aid, Peace, and Justice in Afghanistan*, Bloomfield, CT: Kumarian Press, 2004

Louis Dupree: *Afghanistan*, Princeton University Press, USA, 1980

David Edwards: *Before Taliban: Genealogies of the Afghan Jihad*, Berkeley: University of California Press, 2002

Larry Goodison: *Afghanistan's Endless War: State Failure, Regional Politics, and The Rise of the Taliban*, University of Washington Press, 2002

Michael Griffin: *Reaping the Whirlwind: The Taliban Movement in Afghanistan*, London: Pluto Press, 2003

Peter Hopkirk: *The Great Game*, Oxford: Oxford University Press, 1991

Christina Lamb: *The Sewing Circles of Heart: A Memoir of Afghanistan*, London: Flamingo, 2002

William Maley (editor): *Fundamentalism Reborn? Afghanistan and the Taliban*, London: C. Hurst, 1998

William Maley: *The Afghanistan Wars*, Basingstoke, UK: Palgrave, 2002

Peter Marsden: *The Taliban: War, Religion and the New Order in Afghanistan*, London: Zed Books, 1998

Angelo Rasanayagam: *Afghanistan: A Modern History*, London: I.B. Tauris, 2003

Ahmed Rashid: *Taliban: Islam, Oil and the New Great Game in Central Asia*, London: I. B. Tauris, 2000

Barnett R. Rubin: *The Fragmentation of Afghanistan*, Harvard: Yale University Press, 1995/2002

CHRIS JOHNSON/OXFAM GB

Acknowledgements

The author thanks all those Afghans who over the years have generously shared with her their understandings and knowledge of their country. They are too many to list, but without them this book could not have been written. Thanks go also to those who, even when they were busy, found time to read and comment on the text.

Oxfam in Afghanistan

Oxfam GB has worked in Afghanistan since 1991 to relive poverty, distress, and suffering among a population racked by one of the longest periods of armed conflict in the modern world. Working with local communities, Oxfam seeks to sustain and improve livelihoods and services, while providing emergency assistance in times of immediate crisis.

Oxfam currently works in the north-east of the country, in the province of Badakhshan, in the central mountains, in an area known as Hazarajat, and in the south in the provinces of Zabul and Qandahar. It runs large-scale operational programmes working with village communities, helping people to improve their living conditions and to make their community organisations stronger and more inclusive. Programmes to control erosion, reclaim land, repair irrigation systems, and develop animal husbandry all seek to tackle food shortages, which are a serious problem in all the areas where Oxfam works; the provision of safe drinking water, sanitation programmes, and community-based health education aims to improve the poor standards of health in Afghanistan; while the winter schools programme and adult literacy classes respond to what is always identified as a priority by communities: the need for education. A heavy emphasis is placed on training, with courses in carpentry, masonry, basic engineering skills for supervisors of local projects, and skills for community veterinary workers and traditional birth attendants. All programmes make a particular effort to involve women as well as men. In many of the remote areas where Oxfam works, no other agency is doing this kind of work.

◀ *A village elder on the way to the Anjaman Pass, Badakhshan*

▼ *Ensuring access to clean water is a continuing priority for the Oxfam programme.*

CHRIS JOHNSON/OXFAM GB

In addition to its local projects, Oxfam undertakes advocacy at a national level in conjunction with ACBAR, the Afghanistan NGOs co-ordinating body, in relation to issues arising from its programme work and also matters of more general concern, such as proposed legislation regulating the operation of NGOs.

In recent years Oxfam has operated substantial emergency programmes in response to the drought and the serious earthquakes that have hit Afghanistan. This has involved major new programmes in parts of the country where Oxfam was not previously working, but where there were no other NGOs able to respond to the situation. Oxfam will continue to respond to emergencies as and when they arise – although, with the increased numbers of NGOs now present in Afghanistan, it does not expect to have to do this beyond its own operational areas.

With the new political situation in Afghanistan, Oxfam GB looks forward to working with the government and contributing to the reconstruction of the country and the rebuilding of its war-torn institutions. In this endeavour it hopes to work more and more with local partners. It is also engaged with other members of Oxfam International in developing a joint strategy for Afghanistan.

▼ *Countless relief and development agencies, both international and local, have sprung up in Afghanistan following the fall of the Taliban. Here, agencies advertise their presence in Shamali, north of Kabul.*

CHRIS JOHNSON/OXFAM GB

Index